APR 11 72

May 6, 197

March of America Facsimile Series

Number 5

Divers Voyages

Richard Hakluyt

Divers Voyages Touching the Discoverie of America

by Richard Hakluyt

ANN ARBOR
UNIVERSITY MICROFILMS, INC.
A Subsidiary of Xerox Corporation

Foreword

Divers voyages touching the discouerie of America was printed in London in 1582 with no indication of authorship other than the initials R. H. at the end of the dedication, but the author is known to have been Richard Hakluyt the younger, who later compiled the great collection of voyage literature entitled *The Principall nauigations, voiages and discoueries of the English nation.* Hakluyt's interest in geography and exploration had first been kindled by his older cousin of the same name, a lawyer of the Middle Temple, who was tireless in his own efforts to encourage English colonization of the New World.

Hakluyt's dedication declared his conviction that the time had come for Englishmen to follow the example of the Spanish and Portuguese in taking a share of the new lands, where the idle surplus population of England could be settled. The narratives included in the volume were designed to provide his countrymen with what was known of North America from the Cabot voyages (which he stressed as the basis of English claims), the mythical voyage of the Zeno brothers, Verrazano's exploration and that of Jacques Cartier, and an account of Jean Ribaut's colony in Florida. Hakluyt added the "Booke of Robert Thorne," two lettters exhorting Henry VIII to explore the northern parts of America, because of Thorne's clear statement of an expansionist policy that Hakluyt himself favored. He prefaced his book with a note on the probability of a Northwest Passage and appended two notes prepared by his cousin as instructions for potential colonizers and a list of valuable commodities to be looked for in America. The compilation was thus planned as a manual that would give would-be colonists facts about the lands as yet unclaimed by other nations. It was also designed to encourage them to undertake new ventures by appealing to their love of country and desire for glory and profit and their zeal as Christians to convert heathen peoples. To the younger Hakluyt, a preacher himself, the last motive had the greatest force; in his dedication he expressed the opinion that recent efforts had failed because they were animated more by love of gain than by zeal "for the aduauncement of the kingdome of Christ, and the enlargement of his glorious Gospell."

The publication of *Divers voyages* brought Hakluyt to the attention of Sir Francis Walsingham, Queen Elizabeth's Secretary of State, who commended Hakluyt's efforts and gave him a mission to perform in connection with the projected colony by Sir Humphrey Gilbert. Until his death in 1616 Hakluyt continued to further English colonization with religious zeal by further writings, private persuasion, and active participation in the planning and formation of schemes for settlement of America.

Divers voyages has been reprinted by the Hakluyt Society with an introduction and notes by John Winter Jones (London, 1850). The activities of Hakluyt and his cousin are described in George B. Parks, *Richard Hakluyt and the English Voyages* (New York, 1928) and E. G. R. Taylor, ed., *The Writings and Correspondence of the Two Richard Hakluyts* (2 vols., London, 1935).

Divers Voyages

DIVERS

voyages touching the difcouerie of
America, *and the Ilands adiacent*
vnto the fame, made firft of all by our
Englifhmen, and afterward by the French-
men and Britons:

And certaine notes of aduertifements for obferua-
tions, neceffarie for fuch as fhall heercafter
make the like attempt,

𝔚ith two mappes anneꝛed heereunto foꝛ the
plainer vnderſtanding of the whole
matter.

Imprinted at Lon-

don for Thomas VVoodcocke,
dwelling in paules Church-yard,
at the figne of the blacke beare.

1582.

The names of certaine late writers of Geographie, with the yeere wherein they wrote.

The

The names of certaine late trauay-
lers, both by sea and by lande, which
also for the most part haue written of
their owne trauayles and voyages.

The yere of
our Lorde.

1178   Beniamin Tudelensis a Iewe.

1270   Marcus Paulus a Venetian.

1300   Harton an Armenian.

1320   Iohn Mandeuile knight, englishman.

1380   Nicolaus and Antonius Zeni, venetians.

1444   Nicolaus Conti venetian.

1492   Christopher Columbus a Genoway.

1497   Sebastian Gabot, an egnlishman the sonne of a venetiã.

1497   M. Thorne and Hugh Eleot of Bristowe, englishmen.

1497   Vasques de Gama a portingale.

1500   Gasper Cortercalis a portingale.

1516   Edoardus Barbosa a portingale.

1519   Fernandus Magalianes a portingale.

1530   Iohn Barros a portingale.

1534   Iaques Cartier a Briton.

1540   Francis Vasques de Coronado Spaniarde.

1542   Iohn Gaetan Spaniarde.

1549   Francis Xauier a portingale.

1553   Hugh Willowbie knight, & Richard Chauncellor Eng.

1554   Francis Galuano a portingale.

1556   Stenen and William Burros Englishmen.

1562   Antonie Ienkinson Englishman.

1562   Iohn Ribault a Frenchman.

1565   Andrewe Theuet a Frenchman.

1576   Martin Frobisher Englishman.

1578   Francis Drake Englishman.

1580   Arthur Pet, and Charles Iackmã Englishmen.

1582   Edwarde Fenton, and Luke warde, Englishmen.

1582   Humfrey Gilbert knight, Edward Heyes, and Antonie
      Brigham Englishmen.

A verie late and great probabilitie of a passage, by the Northwest

part of America in 58. degrees
of Northerly latitude.

AN excellent learned man of portingale, of singuler grauety, authoritie and experience tolde mee very lately, that one *Anus Cortereal*, captayne of the yle of Tercera about the yeere 1574. which is not aboue eight yeres past, sent a Shippe to discouer the Northwest passage of America, & that the same shippe arriuing on the coast of the saide America in fiftie eyghte degrees of latitude, founde a great entrance exceeding deepe and broade, without all impediment of ice, into whiche they passed aboue twentie leagues, and found it alwaies to trende towarde the South, the lande lying lowe and plaine on eyther side: And that they perswaded them selues verely, that there was a way open into the south sea. But their victailes fayling them, and being but one shippe, they returned backe agayne with ioy. This place seemeth to lie in equal degrees of latitude, with the first entrance of the sounde of Denmark betweene Norway and the head land, called in latin *Cimbrorum promontorium*, and therefore like to bee open and nauigable a great part of the yeere. And this report may bee well annexed vnto the other eight reasons mentioned in my epistle dedicatorie, for proofe of the likelihood of this passage by the Northwest.

❧ To the right worſhipfull and
moſt vertuous Gentleman maſter
Phillip Sydney Eſquire.

Maruaile not a little (right wor-
ſhipfull)that ſince the firſt diſco-
uerie of America (which is nowe
full foureſcore and tenne yeeres)
after ſo great conqueſts and plan-
tings of the Spaniardes and Portingales there, that wee of Englande could neuer haue the grace
to ſet faſt footing in ſuch fertill and temperate places, as are
left as yet vnpoſſeſſed of them. But againe when I conſider
that there is a time for all men, and ſee the Portingales time to
be out of date, & that the nakedneſſe of the ſpaniards, and their
long hidden ſecretes are nowe at length eſpied , whereby they
went about to delude the worlde, I conceiue great hope, that
the time approcheth and nowe is, that we of England may ſhare
and part ſtakes (if wee will our ſelues) both with the ſpaniarde
and the Portingale in part of America, and other regions as yet
vndiſcouered . And ſurely if there were in vs that deſire to
aduaunce the honour of our Countrie which ought to bee in
euery good man , wee woulde not all this while haue fore-
ſlowne the poſſeſſing of thoſe landes , whiche of equitie
and right appertaine vnto vs, as by the diſcourſes that followe
ſhall appeare moſt plainely. Yea if wee woulde beholde with
the eye of pitie howe al our Priſons are peſtered and filled with
able men to ſerue their Countrie, which for ſmall roberies are
dayly hanged vp in great numbers euen twentie at a clappe out
of one iayle (as was ſeene at the laſt aſſiſes at Rocheſter) wee
woulde haſten and further euery man to his power the deduc-
ting of ſome Colonies of our ſuperfluous people into thoſe temperate and fertile partes of America, which being within ſixe

¶   weekes

weekes ſayling of England are yet vnpoſſeſſed by any Chriſtians?
and ſeeme to offer themſelues vnto vs, ſtretching neerer vnto her
Maieſties Dominions, then to any other part of Europe. Wee
reade that the Bees, whē they grow to be too many in their own
hiues at home, are wont to bee led out by their Captaines to
ſwarme abroad, and ſeeke themſelues a new dwelling place.
If the examples of the Grecians and Carthaginians of olde
time, and the practiſe of our age may not mooue vs, yet let vs
learne wiſdome of theſe ſmal weake and vnreaſonable creatures.
It chaunced very lately that vpon occaſion I had great conference
in matters of Coſmographie with an excellent learned man of
Portingale, moſt priuie to all the diſcoueries of his nation, who
wondered that thoſe bleſſed countries, from the point of Florida Northward, were all this while vnplanted by Chriſtians, pro-
teſting with great affection and zeale, that if hee were nowe as
young as I (for at this preſent hee is threeſcore yeeres of age) hee
woulde ſel all hee had, being a man of no ſmall wealth and honour, to furniſh a conuenient number of ſhips to ſea for the inhabiting of thoſe countries, and reducing thoſe gentile people
to chriſtianitie.   Moreouer hee added that Iohn Barros their
chiefe Coſmographer being moued with the like deſire, was the
cauſe that Breſilia was firſt inhabited by the Portingales: where
they haue nine baronies or lordſhips, & thirtie engennies or ſu-
ger milles, two or three hundred ſlaues belonging to eche myll,
with a Iudge, and other officers, & a Church: ſo that euery mill
is as it were a little common wealth: and that the countrie was
firſt planted by ſuch men, as for ſmall offences were ſaued from
the rope. This hee ſpake not onely vnto mee and in my hearing,
but alſo in the preſence of a friend of mine, a man of great ſkill in
the Mathematikes. If this mans deſire might bee executed, wee
might not only for the preſent time take poſſeſsion of that good
land, but alſo in ſhort ſpace by Gods grace finde out that ſhorte
and eaſie paſſage by the Northweſt, which we haue hetherto ſo
long deſired, and whereof wee haue many good and more then
probable coniectures: a fewe whereof I thinke it not amiſſe
keere to ſet downe, although your worſhip knowe them as
well.

The ſpeech of a learned Portingale.

Maſter John Barros the cauſer of the inhabiting of Breſilia.

well as my selfe. Firſt therefore it is not to bee forgotten, that Se-
baſtian Gabot wrote to maſter Baptiſta Ramuſius, that he very-
ly beleeued that all the North part of America is diuided into I-
landes. Secondly that maſter Iohn Verarzanus, which had been
thriſe on that coaſt, in an olde excellent mappe, which he gaue to
king Henrie the eight, and is yet in the cuſtodie of maſter Locke,
doth ſo lay it out, as it is to bee ſeene in the mappe annexed to
the end of this boke, beeing made according to Verarzanus plat.

Thirdly the ſtory of Gil Gonſalua recorded by Franciſcus Lo-
pes de Gomara, which is ſaide to haue ſought a paſſage by the
Northweſt, ſeemeth to argue and proue the ſame . Fourthly,
in the ſecond relation of Iaques Cartier the 12.Chapter the people of Saguinay doe teſtifie that vpon their coaſtes Weſtwarde
there is a ſea the ende whereof is vnknowne vnto them. Fiftly,
in the end of that diſcourſe is added this, as a ſpecial remembrance, to wit, that they of Canada ſay that it is a monethes
ſpace to ſaile to a lande where cinamon and cloues are growing.
Sixtly, the people of Florida ſignified vnto Iohn Ribault (as it
is expreſſed in his diſcourſe heerewithall imprinted) that they
might ſaile from the Riuer of May vnto Ceuola and the ſouth
ſea through their countrie within twentie dayes . Seuenthly,
the experience of captaine Frobiſher on the hyther ſide, and Sir
Fraunces Drake on the backe ſide of America, with the teſtimonie of Nicolaus and Anthonius Zeni, that Eſtotilanda is an I-
lande, doth yeelde no ſmall hope thereof. Laſtly, the iudgement of the excellent Geographer Gerardus Mercator, which his
ſonne Rumold Mercator my friende ſhewed mee in his letters, &
drewe out for mee in writing, is not of wiſe men lightly to bee
regarded. His words are theſe. *Magna tametſi pauca de noua* The iudgement
Frobiſheri nauigatione ſcribis, quam miror ante multos annos of Gerardus
nõ fuiſſe attentatam. Non enim dubium eſt, quin recta & bre- Mercator of a
uis via pateat in occidentem Cathaium vſq;. In quod regnũ, paſſage by the
ſi recte nauigationem inſtituant, nobiliſſimas totius mundi Northweſt.
merces colligent, & multis Gentibus adhuc idololatris Chriſti
nomen communicabunt. You write (ſaith hee to his ſonne)
great matters though very briefly of the newe diſcouerie

¶ 2   of of Frobisher, which I wonder was neuer these many yeeres heeretofore attempted. For there is no doubt,but that there is a straight and short way open into the West euen vnto Cathay. Into which kingdome, if they take their course aright, they shall gather the most noble merchandise of all the worlde, and shall make the name of Christe to bee knowne vnto many idolatrous and Heathen people. And heere to conclude and shut vp this matter, I haue hearde my selfe of Merchants of credite that haue liued long in Spaine, that King Phillip hath made a lawe of late that none of his subiectes shall discouer to the Northwardes of fiue and fortie degrees of America : whiche may bee thought to proceede chiefly of two causes, the one, least passing farther to the North they should discouer the open passage from the south sea to our north sea : the other because they haue not people enough to possesse and keepe that passage, but rather thereby shoulde open a gappe for other nations to passe that way. Certes if hetherto in our owne discoueries we had not beene led with a preposterous desire of seeking rather gaine then Gods glorie, I assure my self that our labours had taken farre better effecte. But wee forgotte, that Godlinesse is great riches, and that if we first seeke the kingdome of God, al other thinges will be giuen vnto vs, and that as the light accompanieth the Sunne, and the heate the fire, so lasting riches do waite vpon them that are zealous for the aduauncement of the kingdome of Christ, and the enlargement of his glorious Gospell : as it is sayde, I will honour them that honour mee. I truste that nowe being taught by their manifolde losses our men will take a more godly course, and vse some part of their goods to his glorie : if not, he will turne euen their couetousnes to serue him, as he hath done the pride and auarice of the Spaniardes and Portingales, who pretending in glorious words that they made their discoueries chiefly to conuert Infidelles to our most holy faith, (as they say) indeed and truth sought not them, but their goods and riches. Whiche thing that our nation may more speedily & happily performe, there is no better meane in my simple iudgemét then the increase of knowledge in the arte of nauigation, &

breas

A lawe made of late by king. Phillip.

breading of skilfulnesse in the sea men: whiche Charles the Emperour and the king of Spaine that nowe is wisely considering haue in their Contractation house in Siuill appointed a learned reader of the sayde art of Nauigation, and ioyned with him certayne examiners, and haue distinguished the orders among the sea men, as the groomet whiche is the basest degree, the mariner which is the seconde, the master the thirde, and the pilote the fourth, vnto the which two last degrees none is admitted without hee haue heard the reader for a certaine space (which is commonly an excellent Mathematician, of which number were Pedro di Medina which writte learnedly of the art of nauigation, and Alonso di Chauez & Hieronimus di Chauez, whose works likewise I haue seene) and being founde fitte by him and his assistantes, which are to examine matters touching experience, they are admitted with as great solemnitie and giuing of presents to the ancient masters and Pilots, and the reader and examiners, as the great doctors in the Vniuersities, or our great Sergeantes at the law when they proceed, and so are admitted to take charge for the Indies.   And that your worshippe may knowe that this is true, Master Steuen Borrows, nowe one of the foure masters of the Queenes nauie, tolde me that newely after his returne from the discouery of Moscouie by the North, in Queene Maries daies, the Spaniards, hauing intelligence that he was master in that discouerie, tooke him into their contractation house at their making and admitting of masters and pilots, giuing him great honour, & presented him with a payre of perfumed gloues woorth fiue or sixe Ducates.   I speake all this to this ende, that the like order of erecting such a Lecture here in London or about Ratcliffe in some conuenient place, were a matter of great consequence and importance, for the sauing of many mens liues and goods, which nowe through grosse ignorance are dayly in great hazerd, to the no small detriment of the whole realme.   For whiche cause I haue dealt with the right worshipfull sir Frances Drake, that seeing God hath blessed him so wonderfully, he woulde do this honour to him selfe and benefite to his countrey, to bee at the cost to erecte such a lecture: Whereunto in most bountifull maner

The contractatiō house at Siuill.

M. Steuen Borrowes.

A lecture of the art of nauigatiō necessarie for to be erected in London.

¶3   as

The bountiful offer of sir Francis Drake toward furthering the art of Navigation.

at the verie first he answered, that he liked so well of the motion, that he woulde giue twentie poundes by the yeere standing, and twentie poundes more before hand to a learned man to furnish him with instruments and maps, that woulde take this thing vpon him: yea so readie he was that he earnestly requested mee to helpe him to the notice of a fitte man for that purpose, which I, for the zeale I bare to this good actiō, did presently, & brought him one, who came vnto him & conferred with him thereupon: but in fine he would not vndertake the lecture, vnlesse he might haue fourtie pounde a yeere standing, and so the matter ceased for that time: howebeit the worthie and good Knight remaineth still constant, and will be, as he told me very lately, as good as his worde. .. Nowe if God shoulde put into the head of any noble man to contribute other twentie pounde, to make this lecture a competent liuing for a learned man, the whole realme no doubt might reape no small benefite thereby, To leaue this matter & to drawe to an ende, I haue heare right worshipfull in this hastie worke first put downe the title which we haue to that part of America which is from Florida to 67. degrees northwarde, by the

Ihon Gabote and his three sonnes.

letters patentes graunted to Iohn Gabote and his three sonnes, Lewes, Sebastian, and Santius, with Sebastians owne Certificate to Baptista Ramusius of his discouerie of America, and the testimonie of Fabian our own Chronicler. Next I haue caused to bee added the letters of M. Robert Thorne to King Henrie the eight, and his discourse to his Ambassadour doctor Ley in Spaine of the like argument, with the kings setting out of two ships for discouerie in the 19. yere of his raigne. Thē I haue translated the voyage of Iohn Verarzanus from thirtie degrees to Cape Briton, (& the last yeere at my charges, and other of my friendes by my exhortation, I caused Iaques Cartiers two voyages of discouering the grand Bay, and Canada, Saguinay, and Hochelaga to bee translated out of my Volumes, which are to be annexed to this present translation). Moreouer following the order of the map, and not the course of time, I haue put downe the discourse of Nicholaus and Antonius Zenie. The last treatise of Iohn Ribault, is a thing that hath been alreadie printed, but not nowe to be be had, vnlesse I had caused it to be printed againe. The mappe is master Michael Lockes, a man, for his knowledge in diuers languages and especially in Cosmographie, able to doe his countrey good, and worthie in my iudgement, for the manifolde good partes in him, of good reputation and better fortune. This cursorie pamphlet I am ouer bold to present vnto your worshippe : but I had rather want a litle discretion, then to bee founde vnthankful to him, which hath been alwaies so readie to pleasure me and all my name.

    Heere I cease, crauing pardon for my ouer boldnesse, trusting also that your worshippe will continue & increase your accustomed fauour towarde these godly and honourable discoueries.

Your worshippes humble alwayes
to commaunde. R. H.

4

A latine copie of the letters patentes of King Henrie the seuenth, graunted

vnto Iohn Gabote and his three sonnes, Lewes, Sebastian, and Santius for the discouering of newe and vnknowen landes.

Enricus dei gratia rex Angliæ & Franciæ, & dominus hibernia, omnibus ad quos præsentes literæ nostræ peruenerint, salutem. Notum sit & manifestum, quod dedimus & concessimus, ac per præsentes damus & concedimus pro nobis & hæredibus nostris dilectis nobis Ioanni Gaboto ciui Veneciarum, Lodouico, Se-

bastiano, & Santio, filiis dicti Ioannis, & eorum & cuiuslibet eorum hæredibus & deputatis plenam ac liberam authoritatē, facultatem & potestatem nauigandi ad omnes partes, regiones & sinus maris orientalis, occidentalis, & septentrionalis sub banneris, vexillis, & insigniis nostris, cum quinque nauibus siue nauigiis, cuiuscunque portituræ & qualitatis existant, & cum tot et tantis nautis & hominibus quot & quantos in dictis nauibus secum ducere voluerint, suis & eorum propriis sumptibus & expensis, ad inueniendum, discoperiendum, & inuestigandum quascunque insulas, patrias, regiones siue prouincias gentilium & infidelium quorumcunqne in qnacunque parte mundi positas, quæ Christianis omnibus ante hac tempora fuerint incognita. Concessimus etiam eisdem & eorum cuilibet, eorumque & cuiuslibet eorum hæredibus & deputatis ac licentiam dedimus ad affigendum prædictas banneras nostras & insignia in quacunque villa, oppido, castro, insula seu terra firma a se nouiter inuentis. Et quòd prænominatus Ioannes & filii

A   eiusdem

eiusdem seu haredes & eorundem deputati, quascunq; biusmo=
di villis, castra, oppida & insulas a se inuentas, qua subiugari,
occupari, possideri possint, subiugare, occupare, possidere valeāt,
tanquā vasalli nostri, & gubernatores, loca tenentes & deputa=
ti, eorundem dominium, titilum, & iurisdictionem earun=
dem villarum, castrorum, oppidorum, insularum, ac terrā firma
sic inuentorum nobis acquirendo. Ita tamen vt ex omnibus
fructibus, proficuis, emolumentis, commodis, lucris, & obuenti-
onibus ex biusmodi nauigatione prouenientibus prafatus Ioannes & filÿ ac haredes, & eorum deputati teneātur & sint ob=
ligati nobis pro omni viagio suo, toties quoties ad portū nostrū
Bristolliae applicuerint (ad quem omnino applicare teneātur,
& sint astricti) deductis omnibus sūptibus & impensis necessa=
riis per eosdem factis, quintam partem capitalis lucri facti, siue
in mercibus siue in pecuniis persoluere. Dantes nos & concede=
tes eisdē suisq; hardibus & deputatis, vt ab omni solutione cu=
stumarum omniū & singulorum bonorum ac mercium, quas se=
cum reportarint ab illis locis sic nouiter inuentis, liberi sint &
immunes. Et insuper dedimus & concessimus eisdem ac suis haredibus & deputatis, quòd terra omnes firma, iusula, vil=
la, oppida, castra, & loca quacunq; a se inuenta, quotquot ab eis
inueniri contigerit, non possint ab aliis quibusuis nostris subditis frequentari seu visitari, absq; licentia pradictorum Ioannis
& eius filiorum suorumq; deputatorum, sub pana amissionis tā
nauium, quàm bonorum omniū quorumcunq; ad ea loca sic in=
uenta nauigare prasuentiū. Volentes & strictissimé mandan=
tes omnibus & singulis nostris subditis tam in terra quàm in
mari constitutis, vt prafato Ioanni & eius filiis, ac deputatis
bonā assistentiam faciant, & tam in armandis nauibus seu nauigiis, quàm in prouisione quietatis & victualium pro sua pe=
cunia emendorum, atq; aliarum omnium rerum sibi prouiden=
darum pro dicta nauigatione sumenda, suos omnes fauores &
auxilia impertiant. In cuius rei testimonium has literas nostras fieri fecimus patentes: teste me ipso apud Westmonaste-
riū quinto die Martii, anno regni nostri vndecimo.

5. Martii. 1495

The:

Enrie by the grace of GOD king of England, and France, and Lorde of Irelande, to all, to whom these presentes shall come, greeting. Be it knowen that wee haue giuen and granted, and by these presentes doe giue and grant for vs and our heyres, to our well beloued John Gabote citizen of Uenice, to Lewes, Sebastian, and Santius, sonnes of the saide John, and to the heires of them and euery of them, and their deputies, full and free authoritie, leaue, and power to sayle to all partes, countreys and seas of the East, of the West, and of the North vnder our banners and ensignes, with fiue ships, of what burden or quantitie soeuer they be: and as many mariners or men as they will haue with them in the saide ships, vpon their owne proper costes and charges to seeke out, discouer and finde whatsoeuer iles, countreyes, regions, or prouinces, of the heathen and infidelles whatsoeuer they bee, and in what part of the worlde soeuer they be, whiche before this time haue been vnknowen to all Christians. We haue granted to them also and to euery of them, the heires of them, and euery of them and their deputies, & haue giuen them licence to set vp our banners and ensignes in euery village, towne, castel, yle, or maine lande of them newely founde. And that the foresaid John and his sonnes or their heires and assignes may subdue, occupie, and possesse all such townes, cities, castles and yles of them founde, which they can subdue, occupie, and possesse, as our vassailes and lieutenantes, getting vnto vs the rule, title, and iurisdiction of the same villages, townes, castles, and firme lande so founde.

Licence graunted to John Gabot, his sonnes and heires, to discouer vnknowen landes vnder the kings banner.

To subdue and possesse those landes as the kings vassalles.

A 2   Yet

Yet so that the foresaide John and his sonnes and heires, and their Deputies bee holden and bounden, of all the fruites, profites, gaines & commodities growing of such nauigation, for euery their voyage as often as they shall arriue at our port of Bristoll, (at the which port they shall be bounde and holden only to arriue) all manner of necessarie costes and charges by them made being deducted, to pay vnto vs

The fift of all goods to be paid to the king.

in wares or money the fifth part of the Capitall gaine so gotten . Wee giuing and graunting vnto them and to their heires and Deputies, that they shall bee free from all

Freedome from all customes.

paying of customes of all and singuler such merchandize, as they shall bring with them from those places so newely founde.

And moreouer wee haue giuen and graunted to them, their heires and Deputies, that all the firme landes, Iles, Villages, Townes, Castles and places whatsoeuer they

None but they & their allignes may trauaile thither.

be, that they shall chaunce to finde, may not of any other of our subiectes bee frequented or visited without the licence of the foresayd John, his sonnes and their deputies vnder paine of forfayture as well of their shippes, as of all and singuler goods of all them that shall presume to sayle to those places so founde. Willing and most straightly commaunding all and singuler our subiectes as well on lande as on sea appointed officers, to giue good assistace to the aforesaid John and his sonnes and deputies, and that as well in arming and furnishing their ships or vessels, as in prouision of quietnesse, and in buying of victualles for their money and all other thinges by them to be prouided necessarie for the saide nauigation, they doe giue them all their helpe and fauour. In witnesse whereof wee haue caused to bee made these our let-

The 5. of march 1594.

ters patentes. Witnesse our selfe at Westminster the fift day of March in the xi. yeere of our reigne.

¶A

❧ A note of Sebaſtian Gabotes voyage of diſcouerie, taken out of an old

Chronicle written by Robert Fabian ſomtime
Alderman of London, which is in the cuſtodie of
Iohn Stowe Citizen, a diligent ſearcher
and preſeruer of Antiquities.

THIS yeere the King, (by
meanes of a Uenetian whiche
made himſelfe very expert and
cunning in knoweledge of the
circuite of the worlde and I-
landes of the ſame , as by a
Carde and other demonſtrati-
ons reaſonable hee ſhewed)
cauſed to man and victuall a
ſhippe at Briſtowe, to ſearche
for an Ilande, whiche, hee ſaide hee knewe well, was riche
and repleniſhed with riche commodities.   Which Ship
thus manned and victualed at the kinges coſt, diuers merchantes of London ventured in her ſmall ſtockes, being in
her as chiefe Patrone the ſaide Uenetian. And in the companie of the ſaide ſhippe ſapled alſo out of Briſtowe three or
foure ſmall ſhips fraught with ſleight and groſſe merchan-
dizes, as courſe cloth, Caps, Laces, points and other trifles,
and ſo departed from Briſtowe in the beginning of May;
of whome in this Maiors time returned no tidings.

*In the 13. yere
of king Henrie
the vii. 1498.*

Note.

Briſtow.

*William Pur-
chas Maior of
London.*

Of three ſauage men which hee brought home,
and preſented vnto the king in the xvii.
yeere of his raigne.

THis yeere alſo were brought vnto the king three men
taken in the new founde Iland, that before I ſpake of

*Three ſauage
men brought
into England*

A 3

Rawe flesh.
Beastes skins. in William Purchas tinre being Maior. These were clothed in beastes skinnes, and ate rawe fleshe, and spake such speech that no man coulde vnderstand them, and in their demeanour like to bruite beastes, whom the king kept a time after. Of the which vpon two yeeres past after I saw two apparelled after the maner of Englishe men in Westminster pallace, which at that time I coulde not discerne from Englishe men, till I was learned what they were. But as for speech I heard none of them vtter one worde.

Iohn Baptista Ramusius in his Preface to the thirde volume of the nauigations, writeth thus of Sebastian Gabot.

IN the latter part of this volume are put certaine relations of Iohn de Uerarzana a Florentine, and of a great Captaine a Frenchman, and the two voyages of Iaques Cartier a Briton, who sailed vnto the lande set in fiftie degrees of latitude to the north, which is called New France: of the which landes hitherto it is not thoughly knowne whether they doe ioyne with the firme lande of Florida and *nova Hispania*, or whether they be separated & diuided all by Sebastian Gabots letters to Ramusius. the Sea as Ilands: and whether that by that way one may goe by Sea vnto the countrie of Cathaio: as many yeeres past it was written vnto me by Sebastian Gaboto our countrie man Uenetian, a man of great experience & very rare in the art of Nauigation, and the knowledge of CosmoNote.graphie: who sayled along and beyonde this land of Newe Fraunce at the charges of king Henrie the seuenth king of He calleth them Ilands. Englande: And hee tolde mee that hauing sayled a long time West and by North beyonde these Ilandes vnto the latitude of 67. degrees and an halfe vnder the North Pole, and at the 11. day of Iune finding still the open Sea Sebastian Gabot might haue sailed to Cathaio. without any maner of impediment, hee thought verily by that way to haue passed on still the way to Cathaio, which is in the East, and woulde haue done it, if the mutinie of the

shipmaster

shipmaster and marriners had not rebelled and made him to returne homewardes from that place. But it seemeth that God doth yet still reserue this great enterprise for some great Prince, to discouer this voyage of Cathaio by this way: which for the bringing of the spiceries from India into Europe were the most easie and shortest of all other wayes hetherto founde out. And surely this enterprise woulde bee the most glorious and of most importance of all other that can be imagined, to make his name great, & fame immortall to all ages to come, farre more then can bee done by any of all these great troubles and warres, which dayly are vsed in Europe among the miserable Christian people.

This voyage to Cathay reserued by God for some great Prince.

This way the shortest of all others.

This discouery were a most glorious enterprise.

This much concerning Sebastian Cabotes discouerie may suffice for a present tast: but shortly, God willing, shall come out in print all his owne mappes & discourses drawne and written by himselfe, which are in the custodie of the worshipfull master Williã Worthington one of her Maiesties Pensioners, who (because so worthie monumentes shoulde not be buried in perpetuall obliuion) is very willing to suffer them to be ouerseene and published in as good order as may bee, to the encouragement and benefite of our Countrie men.

William Worthington Pensioner.

A declaration of the Indies and landes

discouered, and subdued vnto the Emperour, and the king
of Portugale. And also of other partes of the Indies
and rich Countries to bee discouered, which the worshipfull master Robert Thorne merchant of London (who dwelt long in the City of Siuil in
Spaine) exhorted king Henrie the eight
to take in hande.

MOST EXCELLENT PRINCE.

Experience proueth that naturai-
ly all Princes bee desirous to ex-
tend and enlarge their dominie-
ons and kingdomes. Wherfore
it is not to bee maruelled, to see
them euery day procure ý same,
not regarding any cost, perill,
and labour, that may thereby
chaunce, but rather it is to bee
marueiled, if there be any prince
content to liue quiet with his owne dominions. For surely the people would thinke he lacketh the noble courage and
spirit of all other. The worlde knoweth that the desires
of Princes haue beene so feruent to obtaine their purpose,
that they haue aduentured and proued things to mans coniecture impossible, the which they haue made possible, and also things difficult haue made facil, and thus to obtaine their
purpose haue in maner turned vp and downe the whole
worlde so many times, that the people inhabiting in the farthest regió of the occident haue pursued with great desires,
labours and perils, to penetrate and enter into the farthest
regions of the Orient: And in likewise those people of the
said partes of the Orient haue had no lesse labour and desire
to enter and penetrate into the farthest land of the Occident,
and so following their purchase haue not seased vntill they

B   could

coulde passe no farther by reason of the great Seas. This
naturall inclination is cause, that scarsely it may bee saide
there is any kingdome stable, nor king quiet, but that his
owne imagination, or other Princes his neighbours doe
trouble him. God and nature hath prouided to your Grace,
and to your Gracious progenitors this Realme of Englande, and set it in so fruitefull a place, and within suche limites, that it shoulde seeme to bee a place quiet and aparted
from all the foresaide desires. One speciall cause is, for
that it is compassed with the Sea : by reason thereof it
seemes, this notwithstanding, their desires and noble cou-
rages haue been most commonly like vnto others : and with
marueilous great labours, costes and perilles, they haue tra-
uelled and passed the Seas making warre not onely with
kings and dominions nigh neighbours, but also with them
of farre countries, and so hath wonne and conquered many
riche and faire Dominions, and amplified this your Graces
Realme with great victorie and glory. And also nowe of
late your Grace hauing like courage and desire, & not without iust cause, to enlarge this your kingdome and demaund
your limites and tribute of the French king, which at that
present hee restrained your Grace in person passed with a
great power into France, putting your Graces person to
great paine and labour, and without doubt victoriously you
had conquered the saide Realme of Fraunce, as yee began,
if your aduersarie had not reconciled him, and knowledged
your Graces right and title : and so promised truely to pay
the tribute then due, and fulfill your request in all thinges,
and also desired your Grace for peace, the which of your cle-
mencie you could not refuse.

Nowe I considering this your noble courage and
desire, & also perceiuing that your Grace may at your pleasure, to your greater glory, by a godly meane, with litle cost,
perill, or labour to your Grace or any of your Subiectes,
amplifie and inriche this your saide Realme, I knowe it is
my bounde dutie to manifest this secrete vnto your Grace,
                                                        which

which hitherto as I suppose hath beene hid : which is that Note.
with a small number of shippes there may bee discouered
diuers newe landes and kingdomes, in the whiche without
doubt your Grace shall winne perpetuall glory and your
Subiects infinite profite. To which places there is
left one way to discouer, which is into the North : For that
of the foure partes of the worlde it seemeth three partes are
discouered by other Princes. For out of Spaine they
haue discouered all the Indies and Seas Occidentall, and
out of Portugale all the Indies and Seas Oriental : So
that by this part of the Orient and Occident, they haue
compassed the worlde. For the one of them departing towarde the Orient, and the other towarde the Occident, met
againe in the course or way of the middest of the day, and
so then was discouered a great part of the same Seas and
coastes by the Spaniardes. So that nowe rest to bee discouered the saide North partes, the which it seemeth to
mee, is onely your charge and duetie. Because the situation of this your Realme is thereunto neerest and ap-
test of all other : and also for that you haue alreadie taken Note.
it in hande : And in mine opinion, it will not seeme well
to leaue so great and profitable an enterprise, seeing it may
so easily and with so little coste, labour, and daunger,
bee followed and obteined : Though heeretofore your
Grace hath made theereof a proofe, and founde not the
commoditie thereby as you trusted, at this time it shall
bee no impediment. For there may bee nowe prouided
remedies for thinges, then lacked, and the inconueniences and lettes remooued that then were cause your Graces desire tooke no full effect, which is, the courses to be
chaunged, and followe the aforesaid new courses. And concerning the marriners, shippes, and prouision, an order may
be deuised and taken meete and conuenient much better then
hetherto. By reason whereof, and by Gods grace, no doubt
your purpose shall take effect. Surely the coste heerein
will bee nothing, in comparison to the great profite.

The labour is much lesse, yea nothing at all, where so great honour and glory is hoped for : and considering well the courses, truly the dagger & way is shorter to vs, then to Spaine or Portugall, as by euident reasons appeareth. And nowe to declare some thing of the commoditie and vtilitie of this Nauigation and discouering, it is very cleere and certaine, that the Seas that commonly men say, that without great danger, difficultie and perill, yea rather it is impossible to passe, those same Seas bee nauigable and without any such daunger, but that shippes may passe and haue in them perpetuall cleerenesse of the day without any darkenesse of the night : which thing is a great commoditie for the nauigants, to see at all times rounde about them, as well the safegardes as daungers, and howe great difference it is betweene the commoditie and perilles of other which lease the most parte of euery foure and twentie houres the saide light, and goe in darkenesse groping their way, I thincke there is none so ignorant but perceiueth this more plainely, then it can bee expressed : yea what a vantage shall your Graces Subiects haue also by this light to discouer the strange landes, countries, and coastes, for if they that bee discouered to sayle by them in darkenesse is with great danger, muche more then the coastes not discouered be dangerous to trauell by night or in darkenesse. Yet these dangers or darknesse hath not letted the Spaniardes and Portingals and other, to discouer many vnknowen realmes to their great perill, which considered (and that your Graces Subiectes maye haue the saide lighte) it will seeme your Graces subiects to bee without actiuitie or courage, in leauing to doe this glorious and noble enterprise. For they being past this little way which they named so dangerous, which may bee ii, or iii. leagues before they come to y̆ Pole, and as much more after they passe the Pole, it is cleere that from thence foorth the Seas and landes are as temperat as in these partes, & that then it may be at the will and pleasure of the marriners, to choose whether they will saile vp y̆ coastes

Note.

coastes that bee colde, temperate, oꝛ hot. Foꝛ they being past the pole, it is plaine they maye decline to what parte they list. If they will goe towarde the Oꝛient they shall inioy the regions of all the Tartarians that extende towarde the midday, and from thence they may goe and pꝛoceede to the lande of ẙ Chinas, & from thence to the lande of Cathaio oꝛiental, which is of all the mayne lande most oꝛientall that can bee reckoned from our habitation. And if from thence they doe continue their nauigation, following the coaste that returns towarde the occident, they shall fall in Melassa, and so in all the Indees which we call oꝛientall, and following that way may returne hither by the Cape of Bona Speransa: and thus they shall compasse the whole woꝛlde. And if they will take their course after they be past the pole, towarde the occident, they shall goe in the backe side of the new found lande, which of late was discouered by your Graces subiectes, vntill they come to the backside and South seas of the Indees occidentalls. And so continuing their viage they may returne thoꝛowe the straite of Magallanas to this countrey, and so they compasse also the woꝛlde by that way, and if they goe this thirde way, and after they bee past the pole, goe right towarde the pole Antartike, and then decline toward the lands and Ilands situated betweene the Tropikes, and vnder the Equinoctial, without doubt they shal find there ẙ richest lãds and Ilands of the woꝛlde of Golde, pꝛecious stones, balmes, spices, and other thinges that wee here esteeme most : which come out of strang countreys, & may returne the same way.

By this it appeareth your Grace haue not onely a greate aduantage of the riches, but also your subiectes shal not trauell halfe of the way that other doe, which goe rounde about as afoꝛesaide.

The booke made by the right worship-
full Master Robert Thorne in the yeere 1527. in Siuill to Doctour ley, Lorde ambassadour for King Hen
rie the eight to Charles the Emperour, being an
information of the parts of the world, discouered by him and the King of Portingale: And also of the way to the
Moluccaes by the
north.

Ight noble & reuerende in &c.
I receiued your letters, & haue
procured and sent to knowe of
your seruant, who your Lorde-
ship wrote shoulde bee sicke in
Merchena. I can not there or
els where heare of him, wout
he be returned to you, or gone
to S. Lucar & shipt. I can not
iudge but that of some contagi-
ous sicknes he died, so that the owner of the house for defa-
ming his house woulde bury him secretly, and not be known
of it. For such things haue ofte times happened in this countrey.

Also to write to your Lordshippe of the newe trade
of spicerie of the Emperour, there is no doubt but that the I-
landes are fertile of cloues, nutmegs, mace, and cinnamon:
And that the saide Ilandes, with other there about, abounde
wh gold, Rubies, Diamonds, Balasses, Granates, iacincts &
other stones & pearles, as al other lāds, that are vnder & nere
ŷ equinoctial. For we see, where nature giueth any thing, she
is no nigarde. For as with vs and other, that are aparted
from the sayde equinoctiall, our mettalles be lead, tynne, and
yron, so theirs be golde, siluer, and copper. And as our
fruites and graines be aples, nuttes, and corne, so theirs bee
dates, nutmegges, pepper, cloues, and other spices. And as
wee

wee haue iette, amber, cristall, iasper, and other like stones,
so haue they rubies, diamonds, balasses, saphires, Iacincts,
and other like. And though some say that of such precious
mettals, graines or kind of spices, and precious stones, the a-
boundance and quantitie is nothing so great, as our mettals,
fruites or stones aboue rehearsed: yet if it be well considered,
how the quantitie of the earth vnder the equinoctiall to both
the tropicall lines, (in which space is founde the said golde,
spices and precious stones) to be as much in quantitie, as almost all the earth from the tropickes to both the poles: it can
not be denied but there is more quantitie of the said mettels,
fruites, spices, and precious stones, then there is of the other
mettels and other thinges before rehearsed. And I see
that the preciousnesse of these thinges is measured after the
distance that is betweene vs, and the things that we haue ap-
petite vnto. For in this nauigation of the spicerie was discouered, that these Ilandes nothing set by golde, but set more
by a knife and a naple of yron, then by his quantitie of Golde:
and with reason, as the thing more necessarie for mans seruice. And I doubt not but to them shoulde bee as precious
our corne and seedes, if they might haue them, as to vs
their spices: and likewise the peeces of glasse that heare wee
haue counterfayted are as precious to them, as to vs their
stones: which by experience is seene daylie by them that
haue trade thither. This of the riches of those countries is
sufficient.

Touching that your Lordship wrote, whether it may be
profitable to the Emperour or no, it may be without doubte
of great profit: if as the king of Portingall doch, he woulde
become a marchant, and prouide shippes and their lading,
and trade thither alone, and defende the trade of these Ilands
for himselfe. But other greater busines withholdeth him
from this. But still, as nowe it is begunne to bee occupied, it
woulde come to much. For the ships comming in safetie, there
woulde thither many euery yeere: of whiche to the Emperour is due of all the wares and Iuelles that come from

thence

thence the fift part for his custome cleare without any cost.
And besides this he putteth in euery flote a certayn quantitie
of money, of whiche hee enioyeth of the gaines pounde and
poundes like as other aduenturers doe. In a flote of three
shippes and a carauell that went from this citie armed by
the marchauntes of it, whiche departed in Aprill last past, J
and my partener haue 1400. Ducates that we employed in
the sayde fleete, principally for that two Englishmen friends
of mine, whiche are somewhat learned in Cosinographie,
shoulde goe in the same shippes, to bring mee certaine relation of the situation of the countrey, and to bee experte in the
Nauigation of those seas, and there to haue informations of
many other things, and aduise that J desire to know especially. Seeing in these quarters are shippes, and marriners of
that countrey, and cardes by which they sayle, though much
vnlike ours: that they should procure to haue the said Cards,
and learne howe they vnderstande them, and especially to
know what Nauigation they haue for those Jlandes Northwardes, and Northeastwarde.

For if from the sayde Jlandes the Sea do extende, without
interposition of lande, to sayle from the North poynt
to the Northeast poynt 1700. or 1800. leagues, they should
come to the Newe founde Jlandes that wee discouered, and
so wee shoulde bee neerer to the sayde spicerie by almost
2000. leagues then the Emperour, or the king of Portingal
are. And to aduise your Lordshippe whether of these spiceries of the King of Portingal or the Emperours is neerer,
and also of the titles that eyther of them hath, and howe
our Newe founde landes are parted from it, (for that by
writyng without some demonstration, it were harde to giue
any declaration of it,) J haue caused that your Lordeshippe shall receyue herewith a little Mappe or Carde of
the worlde: the whiche, J feare mee, shall put your Lordshippe to more labour to vnderstande, then mee to make
it, only for that it is made in so little roome that it cannot be
but obscurely set out, ꝑ is desired to be seene in it, ꝗ also for
ꝑ J am in this science litle expert: Yet to remedy in part this
diffi-

difficultie,it is neceffary to declare to your Lordſhippe my
intent,with which I truſt you ſhal perceiue in this card pare
of your deſire,if,for that I cannot expreſſe mine intent, with
my declaratiõ I doe not make it more obſcure.

Firſt, your Lordſhip knoweth that the Coſmographers
haue deuided the earth by 360.degrees in latitude , and as
many in longitude,vnder the which is comprehended al the
roundneſſe of the earth : the latitude beeing deuided into 4.
quarters,ninetie degrees amount to euerie quarter, which
they meaſure by the altitude of the poles, that is the North
and South ſtarres, beeing from the line equinoctiall till
they come right vnder the Noth ſtarre the ſaide ninetie degrees : and aſmuche from the ſayde line equinoctiall to the
South ſtarre bee other ninetie degrees . And aſmuche
more is alſo from eyther of the ſaide ſtarres agayne to the
equinoctiall . Which imagined to be rounde, is ſoone
perceiued thus, 360. degrees of latitude to be conſumed in
the ſaid foure quarters,of ninetie degrees a quarter , ſo that
this latitude is the meaſure of the worlde from North to
South,and from South to North. And the longitude, in
which are alſo counted other 360. is counted frõ Weſt to
Eaſt, or from Eaſt to Weſt, as in the card is ſet.The ſaid
latitude your Lordſhip may ſee marked and deuided in the
end of this carde on the left hande. So that if you woulde To know the
know in what degrees of latitude any region or coaſt ſtan- latitudes.
deth, take a compaſſe and ſet the one foote of the ſame in the
equinoctiall line right againſt the ſaid region, and apply the
other foote of the compaſſe to the ſaide region or coaſt, and
then ſet the ſayd compaſſe at the ende of the carde, where the
degrees are deuided, And the one foote of the cõpaſſe ſtan-
ding in the line equinoctiall,the other will ſhewe in the
ſcale the degrees of altitude or latitude that the ſayd region
is in. Alſo the longitude of the worlde I haue ſet out in the
nether part of the carde , contayning alſo 360. degrees:
which begin to be coũted after Ptolome and other Coſmographers from an head land called *Capo verde*, which is o-
uer againſt a little croſſe made in the part occidentall,where

C the

the diuision of the degrees beginneth, & endeth in ý same *Capo verde.* Nowe to knowe in what longitude any lande is,
your Lordeshippe must take a ruler oz a compasse , and set
the one foote of the compasse vpon the lande oz coast whose
longitude you woulde knowe , and extende the other
foote of the compasse to the nexte parte of one of the transuersall lines in the Ozientall oz Occidentall part : which
done, set the one foote of the compasse in the saide transuersall lyne at the ende of the nether scale , the scale of
longitude, and the other foote sheweth the degree of longitude that the region is in. And your Lordshippe must
vnderstande that this carde though little conteyneth the
vniuersall whole wozlde betwixte the twoo collaterall
lines, the one in the Occidentall parte descendeth perpen-
dicular vppon the 175. degree , and the other in the
Ozientall on the 170. degree , whose distaunce measu-
reth the scale of longitude. And that whiche is without
the two sayde transuersall lynes is onely to shew howe the
Oziental part is ioyned with the Occident, & Occident with
the Ozient. Foz that that is set without the line in the Ozient parte, is the same that is set within the other line in the
Occidentall parte : and againe that that is sette without
the line in the Occidentall part, is the same that is set within the line on the Ozientall parte : To shewe that though
this figure of the wozlde in playne oz flat seemeth to haue
an ende, yet one imagining that this sayde carde were set
vpon a round thing, where the endes shoulde touche by the
lines, it would plainely appeare howe the Ozient part ioyneth with the Occident, as there without the lines it is described & figured. And foz moze declaration of the said carde,
your Lordship shall vnderstand, that beginning on the parte
Occidentall within the lyne, the first land that is set out, is ý
mayne land & Iland of the Indies of ý Emperour. Which
mayne lande oz coast goeth Nozthwarde , and finisheth in
the lande that wee founde, whiche is called heere *Terra de
Labrador.* So that it appeareth the sayde lande that we e
founde and the Indies to bee all one mayne lande. The
sayd.

sayd coast from the saide Indies Southwarde , as by the
carde your Lordshippe may see, cōmeth to a certaine straite
sea called *Estrecho de todos Sanctos*: by which straite Sea Now called the streit of Mage-lane.
the Spaniardes goe to the spiceries , as I shall declare
more at large: the which straite sea is right against the
three hundred fifteene degrees of Longitude , and is of
Latitude or altitude from the Equinoctiall fiftie three degrees. The first lande from the sayd beginning of the carde
towarde the Orient is certaine Ilandes of the Canaries &
Ilandes of *Capo verde*. But the first mayne lande next to
the line Equinoctiall is the sayde *Capo verde* , and from
thence northwarde by the streite of this sea of Italie . And
so followeth Spayne , Fraunce , Flaunders, Almaine,
Denmarke and Norway, which is the highest parte toward the North. And ouer against Flaunders are our Ilands
of England and Irelande. Of the landes and coastes within the straites I haue set out onelye the Regions , deui-
ding them by lynes of their lymittes, by whiche playnelie
I thinke your Lordship may see , in what situatiō euery region is, and of what highnesse, & with what regions it is ioyned. I doe thinke few are lefte out of all Europe . In the
partes of Asia and Affrica I could not so well make the said
diuisions: for that they be not so well knowen, nor neede not
so muche. This I write because in the sayde carde bee made
the sayde lynes and strikes, that your Lordshippe should
vnderstande wherefore they doe serue . Also returning
to foresayde *Capo verde* the coast goeth Southwarde to
a cape called *Capo de bona speransa* : whichis right ouer
agaynst the sixtye and sixtie fifte degree of Longitude .
And by this cape goe the Portingales to their spicerie.
For from this cape towarde the Orient , is the Lande
of Calicut , as your Lordshippe may see in the head lande o-
uer against the 130. degree. From the said cape of *Bona Spe-*
ransa the coast returneth toward the line Equinoctiall, and
passing foorth entreth the read sea, & returning out entreth
againe into the gulfe of Persia , and returneth towarde
the Equinoctiall line , till that it commeth to the head-

lande

land called Callicut afore saide, and from thence the coast making a Gulfe, where is the riuer of Ganges, returneth towarde the line to a head lande called Malacha ; where is the principall spicerie: And from this cape returneth and maketh a great gulfe, and after the coast goeth right toward the Orient, and ouer against this last gulfe and coast be manie Ilandes, which be Ilandes of the spiceries of the Emperour. Upon which the Portingales and he be at variaunce.

Note.

The said coast goeth towarde the Orient, and endeth right against the 155. degrees, and after returneth toward the occident Northwarde: which coast not yet plainely knowne I may ioyn to the new found land found by vs, that I spake of before. So that I finishe with this a briefe declaration of the carde aforesayde. Well I knowe I shoulde also haue declared how the coastes within the streites of the Sea of Italie runne. It is plaine that passing the streites on the Northside of that Sea after the coast of Granado, and with that which pertaynes to Spayne, is the coast of that which Fraunce hath in Italie. And then followeth in one peece all Italie, which lande hath an arme of a sea with a gulfe which is called *Mare Adriaticum*. And in the bottome of this gulfe is the citie of Venice. And on the other part of the said gulfe is Sclauonia, and nexte Grecia, then the streites of Constantinople, and then the Sea called *Euximus*, which is within the saide streites: And comming out of the said straits floweth toward Turcia maior. (Though now on both sides it is called Turcia.) And so the coast runneth Southward to Syria, and ouer against the said Turcia are the Ilades of Rhodes, Candie, and Cyprus. And ouer against Italie are the Ilandes of Sicilia & Sardinia. And ouer against Spaine is Maiorca and minorca. In the ende of the gulfe of Syria is Iudea. And from thence returneth the coast toward the Occident, till it commeth to the streites where wee beganne, whiche all is the coast of Affricke or Barbarie. Also your Lordshippe shall vnderstande that the coastes of the Sea throughout all the world I haue coloured with yellow, for that it may appeare

that

that all that is within the line coloured yellow, is to be imagined to be mayne land or Iland: and all without the sayde
line so coloured to bee Sea: whereby it is easie and light to
know it. Albeit in this little roome any other description
would rather haue made it obscure then cleere. Also the sayd
coasts of the Sea are all set iustly after the manner & forme
as they lye, as the nauigation approoueth the throughout all
the carde, saue onely the coastes and Iles of the spicerie of ÿ
Emperour which is from ouer against the 160. to the 215.
degrees of Longitude. For these coastes & situations of the
Ilands euery of the Cosmographers and pilots of Portingall and Spayne doe set after their purpose. The Spaniards more towards the Orient, because they should appeare
to appertaine to the Emperour: and the Portingalles more
toward the Occident, for that they should fall within their
iurisdiction. So that the Pilots & nauigants thither, which
in such cases should declare ÿ truth, by their industrie doe set
thē falsely euery one to fauour his prince. And for this cause
can be no certaine situatiō of ÿ coast & Ilands, til this difference betwixte them be verified .   Nowe to come to the
purpose of your Lordshippes demaunde touching the difference betweene the Emperour and the king of Portingall,
to vnderstād it better, I must declare ÿ beginning of this discouering . Though peraduēture your Lordship may say ÿ in
that I haue writtē ought of purpose I fall in the Prouerbe,
A gemino ouo bellum: But your Lordship commaunded me
to be large, & I take licence to be prolixouse, & shalbe peraduenture tedious, but your Lordship knoweth that *nihil igno-
rantia verbosius*. In the peere 1484. the king of Portingal
minded to arme certaine caruelles to discouer this spicery.
Then forasmuch as he feared that being discouered euerie
other prince would send & trade thither, so ÿ the cost & peril
of discouering should be his, & the profite common : wherefore first he gaue knowledge of this his mynd to al princes
christened, saying ÿ he would seeke amōgst ÿ infidels newe
possessiōs of regions, & therfore would make a certain army:
& ÿ if any of thē would help in ÿ cost of ÿ said army he should

enioy his parte of the profite or honour that shoulde come
of it . And as then this discouering was holden for a
straunge thing and vncertaine. Nowe they say,that all the
Princes of Christendome aunsweared that they woulde bee
no part of such an army, nor yet of the profite y might come
of it.After the which he gaue knowledge to the Pope of his
purpose,& of the answere of all the Princes,desiring him y
seeing that none would helpe in the costes , that hee woulde
iudge all that shoulde bee founde and discouered to be of his
iurisdiction,and commaund that none other Princes should
intermeddle therewith.The Pope saide not as Christ saith,
Quis me constituit iudicem inter vos? He did not refuse,but
making him selfe as Lorde and Iudge of all, not only graū-
ted that all that should be discouered from Oriēt to Occidēt
shoulde be the kings of Portingall, but also, that vpon great
censures no other Prince should discouer but he: And if they
did,all to be the kinges of Portingall.So he armed a fleete,
and in the yeere 1487.was discouered y Ilands of Calicut,
from whence is brought all the spice he hath. After this in
the yeere 1492. the king of Spaine willing to discouer
landes towarde the Occident without making any such diligence,or taking licence of the king of Portingale, armed
certayne caruelles,and then discouered this India Occidentall , especially two Ilandes of the saide India, that in this
carde I set foorth named the one *Ladominica*, and the other
Cuba,and brought certaine gold from thence.Of the which
when the king of Portingall had knowledge, he sent to the
king of Spayne, requiring him to giue him y said Ilands.
For that by the sentence of the Pope all that should be discouered was his,and that he should not proceede further in the
discouerie without his licence. And at the same time it seemeth that out of Castill, into Portingale had gone for feare
of burning infinite number of Iewes that were expelled out
of Spayne,for that they would not turne to be Christians,&
carried with thē infinite number of gold & siluer.So that it
seemeth that the king of Spayne answered that it was reasō
that the king of Portingall asked , and that to bee obedient
to

that which the pope had decreed, he would giue him the said Ilands of the Indies. Now for as much as it was decreed betwixt ÿ said kings, ÿ none should receiue ÿ others subiects fugitiues, nor their goodes, therefore the king of Portingale should pay and returne to the king of Spaine a million of Golde or more, that the Iewes had carried out of Spaine to Portingale; and that so doing he would giue these Ilandes and desist from any more discouering. And not fulfilling this he would not onely not giue these Ilands, but procure to discouer more where him thought best. It seemeth that the king of Portingale would not or could not with his ease pay this mony. And so not paying that he coulde not let the king of Spaine to discouer: so that hee enterprised not toward the Orient where he had begun and found the spicery. And consented to the king of Spaine that touching this discouering they should deuide the worlde betweene them two. And that all that should be discouered frō *Capo verde*, where this carde beginneth to be counted in the degrees of longitude, to 180, of the sayde scale of longitude, which is halfe the worlde toward the Orient, and finisheth in this carde right ouer against a little crosse made at the sayde 180, degrees, to be the king of Portingalles. And all the lande from the sayde Crosse towarde the Occident, vntill it ioyneth with the other Crosse in the Orient, which conteineth the other hundreth and eightie degrees, that is the other halfe of the worlde, to bee the king of Spaynes. So that from the lande ouer agaynst the sayde hundreth and eightie degrees vntill it finish in the three hundred and sixtie on both the endes of the carde, is the iurisdiction of the king of Spayne. So after this manner they deuided the worlde betweene them. Nowe for that these Ilandes of spicerie fall neere the terme and lymites betweene these Princes (for as by the sayde carde you maye see they beginne from one hundred and sixtie degrees of Longitude, and ende in 215.) it seemeth all that falleth from 160, to 180, degrees, shoulde bee of Portingall:

and

and all the rest of Spayne. And for that their Cosmographers and Pilots could not agree in the situation of the said Ilands (for the Portingals set them al within their 180. degrees, and the Spaniards set them all without: & for that in measuring, all the Cosmographers of both partes, or what other that euer haue beene cānot giue certaine order to measure ẏ lōgitude of the world, as they do of ẏ latitude: for ẏ there is no starre fixed frō East to West, as are ẏ starrs of the poles from North to South, but all mooueth with the mouing diuine:) no māner can be found how certainely it may be measured, but by coniectures, as the Nauigantes haue esteemed the way they haue gone. But it is manifest that Spayne had the situation of all the landes from *Capo verde*, towarde the Orient of the Portingales to their 180. degrees. And in all their cardes they neuer hitherto set the sayd Ilands within their limitatiō of the sayd 180. degrees: (Though they knew very well of the Ilandes,) til nowe that the Spaniards discouered them. And it is knowne that the king of Portingale had trade to these Ilands afore, but would neuer suffer Portingale to goe thither from Calicut: for so much as hee knewe that it fell out of his dominion: least by going thither there might come some knowledge of those other Ilandes of the king of Spayne, but bought the cloues of Merchauntes of that countrie, that brought them to Calicut, much deerer then they would haue cost, if he had set for thē, thinking after this maner it would abide alwaies secrete. And now that it is discouered he sendes and keepes the Spaniards from the trade all that he can. Also it should see me that when this foresaide consent of the diuision of the worlde was agreed of betweene them, the king of Portingale had alreadye discouered certayne Ilandes that lye ouer against *Capo verde*, and also certayne parte of the mayne lande of India towarde the South, from whence he set Brasill, and called it the lande of Brasill. So for that all shoulde come in his terme and limites, hee tooke three hundred and seuentie leagues beyonde

Capo

The longitudes harde to be founde out.

Capo verde: and after this, his 180.degrees, being his part
of the worlde, shoulde beginne in the Carde right ouer a-
gainst the 340 degrees, where I haue made a little compasse with a crosse, and shoulde finishe at the 160.degree,
where also I haue made an other little marke. And after this
computation without any controuersie, the Ilandes of the
spicerie fall out of the Portingales domination. So that
nowe the Spaniardes say to the Portingales that if they
woulde beginne their 180. degrees from the saide Capo
verde, to the intent they shoulde extende more towarde the o-
riente, and so to touche those Ilandes of the spicerie of the
Emperour, which is all that is betweene the two crosses
made in this carde, that then the Ilandes of Capo verde
and the lande of Brasill that the Portingales nowe obtaine,
is out of the sayde limitation, and that they are of the Emperours. Or if their 180. degrees they count from the 370.
leagues beyonde the sayde Capo verde, to include in it the
sayde Ilandes and landes of Brasill, then plainely appeareth the saide 180. degrees shoulde finishe longe before they
come to these Ilandes of the spicerie of the Emperour : As
by this Carde your Lordeshippe may see. For their li-
mittes shoulde beginne at the 340. degrees, of this Carde,
and ende at 160.degrees, where I haue made two little
marks of the compasse with crosses in them.

So that plainely it shoulde appeare by reason, that the
Portingales shoulde leaue these Ilandes of Capo verde and
land of Brasill, if they would haue part of the spicerie of the
Emperours: or else holding these, they haue no parte there.
To this the Portingales say, that they will beginne their
180. degrees from the selfe same Capo verde : for that
it maye extende so muche more towarde the oriente and
touche these Ilandes of the Emperours : and woulde
winne these Ilandes of Capo verde and lande of Brasill neuer the lesse, as a thinge that they possessed before the consent of this limitation was made.

So none can verylye tell whiche hath the best reason.
Thep

They bee not yet agreed, Quandiſub Iudice lis eſt) But without doubte by all coniectures of reaſon the ſayde Ilandes fall all without the limitation of Portingale , and pertayne to Spaine, as it appeareth by the moſt parte of all the Cardes made by the Portingales , ſaue thoſe they haue falſiſied of late purpoſely.   But nowe touching that your Lordſhippe wrote, whether that which wee diſcouered toucheth any thing the foreſayde coaſtes : once it appeareth

plainely that the Newe founde lande that wee diſcouered is all a mayne lande with the Indies occidentall, from whence the emperour hath all the golde and pearles: and ſo continueth of coaſte more then 5000. leagues of length, as by this Carde appeareth.   For from the ſaide newe landes it proceedeth toward the occidēt to the Indies , and from the Indies returneth toward the oriēt,& after turneth ſouthwarde vp till it come to the ſtraytes of Todos Sanctos, whiche I reckon to bee more then 5000. leagues.

New found lãd diſcouered by the engliſhmen.

So that to the Indians it ſhoulde ſeeme that wee haue ſome title , at leaſt that for our diſcouering wee might trade thither as other doe: But all this is nothing neere the ſpicerie.

Note.

Nowe then (if from the ſayde newe founde landes the Sea bee Nauigable,) there is no doubte, but ſayling Northwarde and paſſing the pole deſcending to the equinoctiall lyne wee ſhall hitte theſe Ilandes , and it ſhoulde bee muche more ſhorter way , then eyther the Spaniardes or the Portingales haue.   For wee bee diſtaunt from the pole but 39. degrees, and from the pole to the Equinoctiall bee 90. the which added together bee 129. degrees, leagues 2480. and myles 7440.   Where wee ſhoulde finde theſe Ilandes. And the Nauigation of the Spaniardes to the ſpicerie is, as by this Carde you may ſee , from Spayne to the Ilandes of Canarie, and from theſe Ilandes they runne ouer the lyne Equinoctiall Southwarde to the cape of the mayne lande of Indians, called the Cape of Sainte

To ſayle by the pole,

Au-

Augustine, and from this Cape Southwardes to the
straytes of Todos Sanctos, in the whiche Nauigation to Oz the straites
of Magelan.
the sayde straites is 1706. oz 1800. leagues : and from
these straytes being past them, they returne towarde the
line Equinoctiall to the Ilandes of spicerie, whiche are di-
stante from the sayde straites 4200 oz 4300. leagues.

The Nauigation of the Portingalles to the sayd Ilands
is, departing from Portingale Southwarde towarde the
Capo verde, and from thence to another Cape passing the
lyne equinoctiall called Capo de bona speransa, and from
Portingale to the cape is 1800. leagues, and from this cape
to the Ilandes of spicerie of the Emperour is 2500.
leagues.

So that by this nauigation amounteth all to 4300. leagues.
So that as afore is sayde, if betweene our Newe founde
landes oz Norway, oz Ilande the Seas towarde the north
be Nauigable, wee shoulde goe to these Ilandes a shorter
way by moze then 2000 leagues And though wee went not Note.
to the saide Ilandes, foz that they are the Emperours oz
Kinges of Portingale, wee shoulde by the way, and comming once to the lyne Equinoctiall, finde landes no lesse
riche of Golde and spicerie, as all other landes are vnder the
saide line Equinoctiall: and also shoulde, if wee may passe
vnder the Nozth, enioye the Nauigation of all Tartarie· Benefite to
Englande.

Which should bee no lesse profitable to our commodities
of clothe, then these spiceries to the Emperour, and king of
Portingale.

But it is a generall opinion of all Cosmographers that Obiection.
passing the seuenth clyme, the sea is all ice, the colde so much
that none can suffer it. And hitherto they had all the like opinion that vnder the lyne Equinoctiall foz muche heate the
lande was inhabitable.

Yet since by experience is prooued no lande so much habi= Answere.
table

D 2

Anſwere.

table no2 moze temperate . And to conclude I thinke the ſame ſhoulde bee founde vnder the No2th, if it were expe-rimented . Fo2 as all iudge, *Nihil ſit vacuum in rerum natura:* So I iudge there is no lande inhabitable,no2 Sea innauigable . If I ſhould w2ite the reaſon that p2eſenteth this vnto mee,I ſhoulde bee too p2olixe,and it ſeemeth not requiſite fo2 this p2eſent matter . God knoweth that though by it I ſhoulde haue no great intereſt,yet I haue had and ſtill haue no little minde of this buſineſſe : So that if I had facultie to my will,it ſhoulde bee þ firſt thing that I woulde vnderſtande,euen to attempt, if our Seas No2th-warde bee nauigable to the Pole,o2 no. I reaſon, that as ſome ſickneſſes are hereditarious, & come from the father to the ſonne, ſo this inclination o2 deſire of this diſcouerie I inherited of my father,which with another merchant of B2i-ſtowe named hugh Eliot were the diſcouerers of the newe found lāds,of the which there is no doubt,as now plainly ap-peareth, if the marriners woulde then haue been ruled , and folowed their pilots mind,the lands of the weſt Indies,from whence all the gold commeth,had beene ours.Fo2 all is one coaſte,as by the carde appeareth, and is afo2eſaide . Alſo in this carde by the coaſtes where you ſee C. your Lo2dſhip ſhall vnderſtand it is ſet fo2 Cape o2 head land, where I, fo2 Iland,where P.fo2 Po2t,where R. fo2 Riuer. Alſo in al this little carde I thinke nothing be erred touching the ſituation of the land,ſaue onely in theſe Ilands of ſpicery : which , fo2 that as afo2e is ſayd,euery one ſetteth them after his minde, there can be no certification how they ſtand. I doe not denie, that there lacke many things,that a conſūmate carde ſhould haue,o2 that a right good demonſtration deſireth . Fo2 there ſhould be exp2eſſed all the mouncaines and riuers that are p2incipall of name in the earth , with the names of Po2tes of the ſea,the names of all p2incipall cities, whiche all I might haue ſet, but not in this Carde, fo2 the little ſpace would not conſent.

Your Lo2dſhip may ſee that ſetting only the names almoſt

of

A true opinion.

A voyage of diſcouerie by the pole.

M.Tho2ne and M.Eliot diſco-uerers of New found land.

The cauſe why the weſt Indies were not ours: which alſo Se-baſtian Gabot w2iteth in a1 epiſtle to Bap-tiſt Ramuſius.

of euery region, and yet not of all, the roome is occupied. Many Ilandes are also left out for the saide lacke of roome: the names almost of all portes put to silence, with the roses of the windes or pointes of the compasse : For that this is not for Pilots to sayle by , but a summarie declaration of that which your Lordship commaunded . And if by this your Lordshippe cannot well perceiue the meaning of this carde, of the which I woulde not maruell, by reason of the rude composition of it, will it please your Lordship to aduise mee to make a bigger and a better mappe, or els that I may cause one to bee made. For I knowe my selfe in this and all other nothing perfect, but *Licèt semper discens, nunquam tamen ad perfectam scientiam peruenient.* Also I knowe to set the forme Sphericall of the worlde in *Plano* after the true rule of Cosmographie , it would haue been made otherwise then this is: Howbeit the demonstration shoulde not haue beene so plaine. And also these degrees of longitude , that I set in the lower part of this Card, shold haue been set along by the line equinoctiall, and so then must bee imagined. For the degrees of longitude neare either of the poles are nothing equal in bignes to them in the equinoctiall. But these are set so, for that setting them a long the Equinoctiall, it would haue made obscure a great parte of the mappe. Many other curiosities may be required, which for the nonce I did not set downe , as well for that the intent I had principally was to satisfie your doubt touching the spicerie, as for that I lacke leysure and time . I trust your Lordshippe correcting that which is erred , will accept my good will, which is to do any thing that I maye in your Lordshippes seruice. But from henceforth I knowe your Lordshippe wil rather commaunde me to keepe silence, then to be large, when you shalbe wearied with the reading of this discourse. Iesus prosper your estate and health.

Your Lordshippes Robert
Thorne. 1527.

D3 Also

ALſo this Carde and that which I wꝛite touching the vartaunce betweene the Emperour and the king of Poꝛtingale, is not to bee ſhewed oꝛ communicated there with many of that Courte. Foꝛ though there is nothing in it pꝛeiudiciall to the Emperour, yet it may bee a cauſe of paine to the maker: as well foꝛ that none may make theſe Cardes, but certaine appointed and allowed foꝛ maſters, as foꝛ that peraduenture it woulde not ſounde well to them, that a ſtranger ſhoulde knowe oꝛ diſcouer their ſecretes: and wolde appeare woꝛſt of all, if they vnderſtand that I wꝛite touching ẏ ſhoꝛt way to the ſpicerie by our Seas. Though peraduenture of troth it is not to bee looked too, as a thing that by all opinions is vnpoſſible, and I thinke neuer will come to effect: and therefoꝛe neither heere noꝛ els where is it to bee ſpoken of. Foꝛ to moue it amongſt wiſe men, it ſhoulde bee had in deriſion. And therefoꝛe to none I woulde haue wꝛitten noꝛ ſpoken of ſuch things, but to your Loꝛdſhip, to whome boldly I commit in this all my fooliſh fantaſie as to my ſelfe. But if it pleaſe God that into Englande I may come with your Loꝛdſhip, I will ſhewe ſome coniectures of reaſon though againſt the gene= rall opinion of Coſmographers, by which ſhall ap= peare this that I ſay not to lacke ſome foundation. And tyll that time I beſeeche your Loꝛdſhip let it bee put to ſilence: and in the meane ſeaſon it may pleaſe God to ſende our two Engliſhmen, that are gone to the ſpicerie, which may alſo bꝛing moꝛe plaine declaration of ẏ which in this caſe might bee deſired. Alſo I knowe it needed not to haue beene ſo pꝛolixe in the declaration of this Carde to your Loꝛdſhip, if the ſaide Carde had beene very well made after the rules of Coſmographie. Foꝛ your Loꝛdſhip woulde ſoone vnder= ſtande it better then I, oꝛ any other that coulde haue made it: and ſo it ſhoulde appeare that I ſhewed *Delphinum nata= re.* But foꝛ that I haue made it after my rude maner, it is ne= ceſſarie that I be the declarer oꝛ gloſer of mine owne woꝛk, oꝛ els your Loꝛdſhip ſhould haue had much labour to vn=

derſtande it, which nowe with it alſo cannot bee excuſed, it is ſo groſſely done. But I knewe you looked for no curious things of mee, and therefore I truſt your Lordſhippe will accept this, and holde mee for excuſed. In other mens letters that they write they craue pardon that at this preſent they write no larger: but I muſt finiſh, aſking pardon that at this preſent I write ſo largely. Ieſus preſerue your Lordſhip with augmentation of dignities.

Your ſeruant Robert Thorne, 1527.

This exhortation to king Henrie the eight, with the diſcourſe to Doctor Ley his Ambaſſadour in Spaine, was preſerued by one maſter Emmanuel Lucar executour to maſter Robert Thorne, and was friendly imparted vnto mee by maſter Cyprian Lucar his ſonne an honeſt Gentleman and very forwarde to further any good and laudable action. And that it may bee knowne that this motion tooke preſent effect with the king, I thought it good herewithall to put downe the teſtimonie of our Chronicle that the king ſet out ſhippes for this diſcouerie in his life time. maſter Hall and maſter Grafton in their Chronicles write both thus: This ſame moneth king Henry the eight ſente two faire ſhips, well manned and victualed, hauing in them diuers cunning men, to ſeeke ſtrange regions: and ſo they ſet foorth, out of the Thames the xx. day of May in the xix. yeere of his raigne. In the yeere of our Lorde. 1527.

FINIS.

❧ To the moſt Chriſtian king of *Fraunce,* Fraunces *the firſt.*

The relation of Iohn Verarzanus a Florentine, of the lande by him diſcouered in the name of his Maieſtie, written in *Diepe* the eight of Iuly 1524.

Wrote not to your Maieſtie (moſt Chriſtian king) ſince the time wee ſuffered the tempeſt in the North partes, of the ſucceſſe of the foure Ships, which your Maieſtie ſent forth to diſcouer new lands by the Ocean, thinking your Maieſtie had been alreadie duly enformed thereof. Nowe by theſe preſents I will giue your Maieſtie to vnderſtand, howe by the violence of the windes wee were forced with ẙ two ships, the Norman and the Dolphin, in ſuch euill caſe as they were, to lande in Britaine. Whereafter wee had repaired them in all pointes as was needefull and armed them very well, wee tooke our courſe along by the coaſt of Spaine. Afterwardes with the Dolphin alone, wee determined to make diſcouerie of newe Countries, to proſecute the nauigation wee had alreadie begun, which I purpoſe at this preſent to recount vnto your Maieſtie, to make manifeſt the whole proceeding of the matter. The 17 of Ianuarie, the yeere 1524. by the grace of God, wee departed from the diſhabited Rocke, by the Iſle of Madêra, appertaining to the king of Portingall, with fiftie men, with victuals, weapon, and other ship munition very well prouided and furniſhed for 8. monethes: And ſayling weſtwards with a faire Eaſterly winde, in 25. dayes wee ranne 500. leagues, and the 20. of Febꝛuarie wee were ouertaken with as ſharpe and terrible a tempeſt as euer any ſaylers ſuffered: whereof with ẙ diuine helpe & mercifull aſſiſtaunce of Almightie God, and the goodneſſe of our ship accompanied

A   with

with the good hap of her fortunate name wee were deliuered,and with a prosperous wind followed our course West
& by North. And in other 25.dayes wee made aboue 400.
leagues more,where wee discouered a newe land,neuer before seene of any man either auncient or moderne,and at the
first sight it seemed somewhat lowe, but beeing within a
quarter of a league of it, wee perceiued by the great fiers
that wee sawe by the Sea coaste that it was inhabited: and
saw that the lande stretched to the Southwards :in seeking
some conuenient harborough whereby to come a lande, and
haue knowledge of the place, wee sayled fiftie leagues in
vaine,and seeing the lande to runn still to the Southwards
wee resolued to returne backe againe towardes the North,
where we found our selues troubled with the like difficulty:
at length beeing in despaire to finde any port, wee caste
anker vpon the coast,and sent our Boate to shore, where we
sawe great store of people which came to the Sea side, and
seeing vs to approche they fled away, and sometimes would
stande still and looke backe, beholding vs with great admiration: but afterwardes beeing animated and assured with
signes that wee made them,some of them came harde to the
Sea side seeming to reioyce very muche at the sight of vs,
and marueiling greatly at our apparell,shape and whitenes,
shewed vs by sundry signes where wee might most commodiously come a land with our Boat,offering vs also of their
victuals to eate . Nowe I will briefly declare to your
Maiestie their life and manners, as farre as wee coulde
haue notice thereof : These people goe altogeather naked
except only that they couer their priute partes with certaine
skinnes of beastes like vnto Marterns, which they fasten
vnto a narrowe girdle made of grasse verye artificially
wrought,hanged about with tailes of diuers other beastes,
which rounde about their bodies hang dangling downe to
their knees. Some of them weare garlandes of byrdes
feathers. The people are of colour russet , and not
much vnlike the Saracens, their hayre blacke, thicke and
not

not very long, which they tye togeather in a knot behinde & weare it like a taile. They are wel featured in their limbs, of meane stature and commonly somewhat bigger then we, brode breasted, strong armes, their legges and other partes of their bodies well fashioned, and they are disfigured in nothing sauing that they haue somewhat brode visages, and yet not all of them: for wee sawe many of them well fauoured hauing blacke and great eyes, with a cheerefull and stedie looke, not strong of body yet sharpe witted, nymble and great runners, as farre as we coulde learne by experience, and in those two last qualities they are like to the people of the East partes of the worlde, and especially to them of the vttermost partes of China, wee coulde not learne of this people their manner of liuing, nor their particuler customes by reason of ⨍ short abode we made on the shore, our companie being but small, and our ship ryding farre of in the Sea. And not farre from these we founde an other people, whose liuing wee thinke to bee like vnto theirs, (as heereafter I will declare vnto your Maiestie,) shewing at this present the situation and nature of the foresaide lande: The shore is all couered with small sande, and so ascendeth vpwardes for the space of fifteene foote rising in forme of little hilles about fiftie paces broade. And sayling forwards wee founde certaine small Riuers and armes of the Sea, that enter at certain creekes, washing the shore on both sides as the coast lyeth. And beyonde this wee sawe the open Countrie rising in height aboue the sandie shore with many fayre fieldes and plaines, full of mightie great woods, some verie thicke and some thinne, replenished with diuers sortes of trees, as pleasaunt and delectable to beholde as is possible to imagine. And your Maiestie may not thinke that these are like the woodes of Hercinia or the wilde Desertes of Tartary, and the Northerne Coastes full of fruitelesse trees: But full of Palme trees, Bay trees, and high Cypresse trees, and many other sortes of trees vnknowne in Europe, which yeeld most sweete sauours farre from the shore, the propertie whereof wee coulde not learne

A 2

For the caufe aforefaide, and not for any difficultie to paffe through the woods: Seeing they are not fo thicke but that a man may paffe through them. Neither doe wee thinke that they part taking of the Eaft worlde rounde about them are all to geather voide of drugs or fpicerie, and other richeffe of golde, feeing the colour of the lande doth fo much argue it. and the lande is full of many beaftes, as Stags, Deare and Hares, and likewife of Lakes and Pooles of Frefh water, with great plentie of foules, conuenient for all kinde of pleafant game. This lande is in latitude 34. D. with good and holfome ayre, temperate, betweene hot and colde, no vehement windes doe blowe in thofe Regions, and thofe that doe commonly raigne in thofe Coaftes, are the North Weft and Weft windes in the Sommer feafon, (in the beginning whereof wee were there) the fkie cleere and faire with very little raine: and if at any time the ayre bee cloudie and miftie with the Sowtherne winde immediately it is diffolued and waxeth cleare and fayre agayne. The Sea is caulme, not boyfterous, the waues gentle, and although all the fhore bee fomewhat lowe and with out harborough: yet it is not daungerous to the faylers beeing free from rockes and deepe, fo that within foure or fiue foote of the fhore, there is twentie foote deepe of water without ebbe or flood, the depth ftill increafing in fuch vniforme proportion. There is very good ryding at Sea: for any Ship beeing fhaken in a tempeft can neuer perifhe there by breaking of her cables, which wee haue proued by experince. For in the beginning of March (as is vfuall in all Regions) beeing in the Sea oppreffed with Northerne windes and riding there, wee founde our anker broken before the earth fayled or mooued at all. Wee departed from this place ftill running a long the coafte, which we found to trende towarde the Eaft, and wee faw euerie where verie great fiers, by reafon of the multitude of the inhabitants. While we rode on that Coafte partlie becaufe it had no harborough, and for that wee wanted water, wee fent our Boat a fhore with

Gr. 34.

with 25.men: where by reason of great and continual waues that beate against the shore, being an open coast, without succour, none of our men coulde possible goe a shore without loosing our boate. We sawe there many people which came vnto the shore, making diuers signes of friendship, and shewing that they were content wee shoulde come a lande, and by trial we found thē to be very courteous & gentle as your maiestie shal vnderstand by the successe. To the intent we might sende them of our thinges, which the Indians commonly desier and esteeme as sheetes of Paper, glasses, belles, and such like trifles : Wee sent a young man one of our Marriners a shore, who swimming towards them, and being within 3. or 4. yeards off the shore, not trusting them, cast the thinges vpon the shore, seeking afterwardes to returne, hee was with such violence of the waues beaten vpon the shore, that he was so bruised that hee lay there almost dead, whiche the Indians perceiuing, ranne to catche him, and drawing him out they carried him a little way off from the sea: The young man perceiuing they caried him, beeing at the first dismaide, began then greatly to feare and cried out pitiously, likewise did the Indians which did accompanie him, going about to cheere him and giue him courage, and then setting him on the grounde at the foote of a little hill against the sunne, beganne to beholde him with great admiration, marueiling at the whitenesse of his fleshe: And putting off his clothes they made him warme at a great fire, not without our great feare which remained in the boate, that they would haue rosted him at that fire and haue eaten him. The young man hauing recouered his strength, and hauing stayed a while with them, shewed them by signes that hee was desirous to returne to the shippe: And they with great loue clapping him fast about with many embracings, accompanying him vnto the sea, and to put him in more assurance, leauing him alone they went vnto a high grounde and stoode there, beholding him vntil he was entred into the boate. This yong man obserued as we did also, that these are of colour enclining to Blacke as the other were, with their fleshe ve-

rie

rie fhining of meane ftature, handfome vifag, and dilicate limmes and of verie little ftrength:but of prompt witte, farther wee obferued not.

Departing from hence following the fhore which trended fomewhat towarde the North in 50.leagues fpace, wee came to another lande which fhewed much more faire and full of woods,being very great, where we rode at Ancker, and that wee might haue fome knowledge thereof, wee fent 20.men a lande, which entred into the countrey about two leagues,and they founde that the people were fledde to the woods for feare, they fawe onely one olde woman with a young maide of 18.or 20.yeeres olde,which feeing our companie hid them felues in the graffe for feare,the olde woman caried two Infantes on her fhoulders,and behinde her necke a childe of 8.yeeres olde : the yong woman was laden likewife with as many:but when our men came vnto them, the women cryed out,the olde woman made fignes that the men were fled vnto the woods, as foone as they fawe vs to quiet them and to winne their fauour, our men gaue them fuche victuals as they had with them to eate,which the old woman receiued thankfully:but the yong woman difdained them al, and threwe them difdainefully on the grounde, they tooke a childe from the olde woman to bring into Fraunce, and going about to take the young woman which was verye beawtifull & of tal ftature, they could not poffibly for y great outcries that fhee made bring her to the fea, and efpecially hauing great woods to paffe through, and being farre from the fhippe,wee purpofed to leaue her behinde bearing away the childe onely. We found thofe folkes to bee more white than thofe that we founde before, being clad with certaine leaues y hang on boughes of trees, which they fowe together with thredes of wilde hempe, their heads were truffed vp after the fame manner as the former were, their ordinarie foode is of pulfe,whereof they haue great ftore, differing in colour & tafte from ours,of good & plafant tafte . Moreouer they liue by fifhing & fouling which they take with ginnes, and bowes made of hard wood the arrowes of Canes,being

hea-

headed with the bones of fishe and other beastes. The beastes
in these parts are much wilder then in our Europe, by reason
they are continually chased and hunted. Wee sawe many of
their boates made of one tree 20. foote long , and 4. foote
broade, which are not made with Iron, or stone, or any other
kinde of metal, (because that in all this countrie for the space
of 200. leagues whiche we ranne, wee neuer sawe one stone
of any sort): they help themselues with fyre, burning so much
of the tree as is sufficient for the hollownesse of the boate, the
like they doe in making the sterne and the foreparte vntill it
be fitte to saile vpon the sea. The lande is in situation, goodnesse and fairenes like the other: it hath woods like the other,
thinne and full of diuers sortes of trees: but not so sweete because the countrey is more northerly and cold.

Wee sawe in this Countrey many Uines growing naturally, which growing vp take hold of the trees as they do
in Lombardie, w̃ if by husbandmen they were dressed in good
order, without all doubte they woulde yeelde excellent
wines : for wee hauing oftentymes seene the fruite thereof dried, whiche was sweete and pleasaunt, and not differing from ours. Wee doe thinke that they doe esteeme
the same, because that in euery place where they growe, they
take away the vnder braunches growing rounde about, that
the fruite thereof may ripen the better.

We found also roses, violettes, lillies, and many sorts of
herbes, and sweete and odoriferous flowers different from
ours. We knewe not their dwellinges, because they were
farre vp in the lande, and wee iudge by manye signes that
wee sawe, that they are of wood and of trees framed together.

Wee doe beleeue also by many coniectures and signes,
that many of them sleeping in the fieldes, haue no other couer then the open skye. Further knowledge haue wee not
of them, we thinke ỹ all the rest whose countreys we passed
liue all after one manner , hauing our aboade three dayes
in this cuntrey, riding on the coast for want of harboroughs.

we con-

concluded to departe from thence, trending along the fhoze betweene the Nozth and the Eaſt, ſayling onely in the day time, & riding at ancker by night in the ſpace of 100.leagues ſayling,wee founde a very pleaſant place, ſituated amongſt certaine litle ſteepe hilles : from amiddeſt the which hilles there ran down into the ſea a great ſtreame of water, which within the mouth was very deep,& from ẙ ſea to ẙ mouth of ſame with the tyde which wce found to riſe 8.foot,any great veſſell laden may paſſe vp.

But becauſe wee rode at Ancker in a place well fenſed from the winde,wee woulde not venture our ſelues without knowledge of the place, and wee paſſed vp with our boate onely into the ſayde Riuer, and ſawe the Countrey very wel peopled.The people are almoſt like vnto the others,and clad with the fethers offoules of diuers colours, they came to wardes vs very cherefully, making great ſhowtes of admi ration,ſhewing vs where we might come to lande moſt ſafe ly with our boate.Wle entred vp the ſaid riuer into the lande about halfe a league, where it made a moſt pleaſant lake a bout 3.leagues in compaſſe: on the which they rowed from the one ſide to the other to the number of 30. of their ſmall boates:wherein were many people whiche paſſed from one ſhoze to the other to come and ſee vs, and beholde vpon the ſodaine(as it is wont to fall out in ſayling)a contrarie flawe of winde comming from the ſea, wee were enfozced to re turne to our Shippe, leauing this lande to our great diſ contentment, foz the great commoditie and pleaſantneſſe

The pleaſant nes and riches of the lande.

thereof whiche wee ſuppoſe is not without ſome ri ches,all the hills ſhewing minerall matters in thẽ.Wle wet ed Ancker,and ſayled towarde the Eaſt, foz ſo the coaſt tren ded,and ſo alwayes foz 50.leagues being in the ſight ther e

The deſcriptiõ of Claudia Iꝫ lande.

of wee diſcouered an Ilande in fozme of a triangle, diſ tant from the maine lande 3.leagues, about the bigneſſe of the Ilande of the Rodes, it was full of hilles couered with trees, well peopled, foz we ſawe fires all along the coaſte,

Claudia was wife of King Francis.

wee gaue the name of it,of your Maieſties mother, not ſtay ing there by reaſon of the weather being contrarie.

And

And wee came to another lande being 15.leagues distant from the Ilande, where wee founde a passing good hauen, wherein being entred we founde about 20. small boates of the people which with diuers cries and wondrings came about our shippe, comming no nerer then 50. paces towards vs,they stayed and behelde the artificialnesse of our ship, our shape & apparel,thã they al made a loud showte together declaring that they reioyced: when we had somethiug animated them vsing their geastes, they came so neere vs that wee cast them certaine bells and glasses and many toyes,whiche when they had receiued they lookte on them with laughing & came without feare aborde our ship.There were among st these people 2.kings of so goodly stature and shape as is possible to declare, the eldest was about 40.yeeres of ag,the second was a yong man of 20.yeres old. Their apparell was on this maner,the elder had vpõ his naked body a harts skin wrought artificialie with diuers braunches like Damaske, his head was bare with the haire tyed vp behinde with diuers knottes: About his necke he had a large chaine, garnished with diuers stones of sundrie colours the young man was almost appareled after the same manner. This is the goodliest people and of the fairest conditions that wee haue found in this our voyage.They exceed vs in bignes,they are of the colour of brasse,some of thẽ encline more to whitnes: others are of yellowe colour, of comely visage with long & blacke heire which they are very carefull to trim and decke vp,they are blacke and quicke eyed.I write not to your Maiestie, of the other parte of their bodie, hauing all suche proportion as appertayneth to anye handsome man. The women are of the like conformitie and Beawtie,verie handsome and well fauoured, they are as well mannered and continente as anye women, of good education , they are all naked saue their priuie partes whiche they couer with a Deares skinne braunched or embrodered as the men vse: there are also of them whiche weare on their armes verie riche skinnes of leopardes, they adorne their heades with diuers ornamentes made of their owne heire, whiche hange

The Countre of Sir H.G. voyage.

B   downe

downe before or both ſides their breſtes, others vſe other
kinde of dreſſing them ſelues like vnto the women of Egypt
and Syria, theſe are of the elder ſorte: and when they are
married they weare diuers toyes, according to the vſage of
the people of the Eaſt as well men as women.

Among whom wee ſawe many plates of wrought coper,
which they eſteeme more then golde, whiche for the colour
they make no accompt of, for that among all other it is
counted the baſeſt, they make moſt accompt of Azure and
red. The things that they eſteemed moſt of al thoſe which we
gaue them were bels, criſtall of Azure colour, and other toies
to hang at their eares or about their necke. They did not deſire cloth of ſilke or of golde, muche leſſe of any other ſorte,
neither cared they for thinges made of ſteele and Iron, which
wee often ſhewed them in our armour whiche they made no
wonder at, and in beholding them they onely aſked the arte
of making them: the like they did at our glaſſes, which whē
the behelde, they ſodainely laught and gaue them vs againe.
They are very liberal for they giue that which they haue, we
became great friendes with theſe, and one day wee entred into the hauen with our ſhippe, where as before wee rode a
league of at ſea by reaſon of the contrary weather. They
came in great companies of their ſmall boates vnto the ſhip
with their faces all be painted with diuers colours, ſhewing
vs ẏ it was a ſigne of ioy, bringing vs of their victuals, they
made ſignes vnto vs where wee might ſafeſt ride in the hauen for the ſafegarde of our ſhippe keeping ſtill our companie: and after we were come to an Ancker, we beſtowed fifteene dayes in prouiding our ſelues many neceſſary things,
whether euery day the people repayred to ſee our ſhip bringing their wiues with them, whereof they are very ielous:
and they themſelues entring abrode the ſhippe and ſtayinge
there a good ſpace, cauſed their wiues to ſtay in their boates,
and for al the intreatie we could make, offering to giue them
diuers things, we could neuer obtaine that they would ſuffer
them to come aborde our ſhip. And oftentimes one of the
two kings comming with his queene, and many gentlemen
for their pleaſure to ſee vs, they all ſtayed on ẏ ſhore two hun-

dred paces from vs, sending a smal boate to giue vs intelligence of their comming, saying they would come to see our shippe, this they did in token of safetye, and assoone as they had answere from vs they came immediatly, and hauing stayed a while to beholde it, they wondered at hearing the cryes and noyes of the marriners. The queene and her maids stayed in a very light boate, at an Iland a quarter of a leage off, while the king abode a long space in our ship vttering diuers conceites with geastures, viewing with great admiration, all the furniture of the shippe, demaunding the propertie of euerie thing perticularly. He tooke likewise great pleasure in beholding our apparell, and in tasting our meates, and so courteously taking his leaue departed. And sometimes our men staying for two or three dayes on a litle Ilande nere the ship for diuers necessaries, (as it is ye vse of seamen) he returned with 7. or 8. of his gentlemen to see what we did, and asked of vs oft times if wee meant to make any long aboade there, offering vs of their prouision: then the king drawing his bowe and running vp and downe with his gentlemen, made much sporte to gratifie our men, wee were oftentimes within the lande 5. or 6. leagues, which we found as pleasant as is possible to declare very apt for any kinde of husbandry of corne, wine and oyle: for that there are plaines 25. or 30. leagues broad, open and without any impediment of trees of such fruitfulnesse, that any seede being sowne therein, will bring forth most excellent fruite. We entred afterwards into the woods which wee found so great and thicke, that any armie were it neuer so great might haue hid it selfe therein, the trees whereof are okes, cipres trees, and other sortes vnknowen in Europe. We found Pomi appii, Damson trees, and Nutte trees, and many other sorts of fruits differing from ours: there are beasts in great abundance, as hartes, deares, leopardes, and other kinds which they take with their nets & bowes which are their chiefe weapons, the arrowes whiche they vse are made with great cunning, and in steade of iron, they head them with smeriglio, wt iasper stone, & hard marble & other sharp stones which they vse in stead of iron to cut

trees,

trees, and make their boates of one whole piece of wood, making it hollowe with great and wonderfull art, wherein 10.
or 12. men may bee commodiously, their oares are shorte and
broad at the ende, and they vse them in the sea without anye
daunger, and by maine force of armes, with as great speedi-
nesse as they liste them selues. We sawe their houses made
in circuler or rounde fourme 10. or 12. foote in compasse,
made with halfe circles of timber, seperate one from another without any order of building, couered with mattes of
strawe wrought cunningly together, which saue them from
the winde and raine, and if they had the order of building and
perfect skil of workmanship as we haue: there were no doubt
but y they would also make eftsoones great and stately buildings. For all the sea coastes are full of cleare and glistering
stones, and alablaster, and therefore it is full of good hauens
and harbarours for ships. They mooue the foresaide houses
from one place to another accordyng to the commoditie of
the place and season wherein they will make their aboade,
and only taking of the couer, they haue other houses builded
incontinent. The father and the whole familie dwell together in one house in great number : in some of them we sawe
25. or 30. persons. They feede as the other doe aforesaide of
pulse whiche doe growe in that countrey with better order
of husbandry then in the others. They obserue in their sowing
the course of the Moone and the rising of certaine starres,
and diuers other customes spoken of by antiquitie. Moreouer, they liue by hunting and fishing. they liue long, and are
seldome sicke , and if they chaunce to fall sicke at any time,
they heale them selues with fire without any phisition, and
they say that they die for very age. They are very pitiful and
charitable towardes their neighbours, they make great la-
mentations in their aduersitie & in their miserie, the kinred
recken vp all their felicitie, at their departure out of life, they
vse mourning mixt with singing, which continueth for a long space.
This is asmuch as wee coulde learne of them. This lande is
situated in the Paralele of Rome, in 41. degrees & 2. terces:
but

but somewhat more colde by accidentall cause and not of nature,(as I will declare vnto your highnesse els where) describing at this present the situation of the foresaide countrie, which lyeth East and West, I say that the mouth of the hauen lyeth open to the South halfe a league broade, and being entred within it betweene the East and the North, it stretcheth twelue leagues: where it waxeth broder and broder, and maketh a gulfe aboute 20. leagues in compasse, wherein are fiue small Islandes very fruitfull and pleasant, full of hie and broade trees, among the which Ilandes, any great Nauie may ryde safe without any feare of tempest or other daunger. Afterwardes turning towards the South and in the entring into the Hauen on both sides there are most pleasant hilles, with many riuers of most cleere water falling into the Sea.

In the middest of this entraunce there is a rock of free stone growing by nature apt to builde any Castle or Fortresse there, for the keeping of the hauen. The fift of May being furnished with all thinges necessarie, we departed from the said Coast keeping along in the sight thereof, & we sayled 150 leagues finding it all wayes after one manner: but the lande somewhat higher with certaine mountaines all which beare a shewe of minerall matter, wee sought not to lande there in any place, because the weather serued our turne for sayling: but wee suppose that it was like to the former, the Coast ranne Eastward for the space of fiftie leagues. And trending afterwardes the North, wee founde another lande high full of thicke woods, the trees whereof were firres, Cipresses and such like as are wont to growe in colde Countries. The people differ much from the other, & looke how much the former seemed to be courteous and gentle: so much were these full of rudenesse and ill manners, and so barbarous that by no signes that euer wee coulde make, wee could haue any kinde of trafficke with them. They cloth themselues with Beares skinnes and Leopardes and sealles and other beastes skinnes. Their foode as farre as wee coulde percieue,

B.5

ceiue, repayring often vnto their dwellings wee suppose to bee by hunting and fishing, and of certaine fruites, which are a kinde of rootes, which the earth yeeldeth of her owne accord. They haue no graine, neither sawe wee any kinde or signe of tyllage, neither is the lande, for the barrennes therof apt to beare frute or seed. If at any time we desired by exchaunge to haue any of their commodities, they vsed to come to the Sea shore vpon certaine craggie rocks, and wee standing in our Boats, they let downe with a rope what it pleased them to giue vs, crying continually that wee should not approch to the lande, demanding immediately the exchange taking nothing but kniues, fishookes and tooles to cut withall, neither did they make any account of our curtesie. And when we had nothing left to exchange with them, when we departed from them the people shewed all signes of discourtesie and disdaine, as was possible for any creature to inuent. Wee were in despight of them two or three leagues within the lande, being in number 25, armed men of vs: And when wee went on shore they shot at vs with their bowes, making great outcries, and afterwardes fled into the woods. Wee founde not in this lande any thing notable, or of importance, sauing very great woods and certaine hilles, they may haue some mynerall matter in them, because wee sawe many of the haue beadstones of Copper hanging at their eares. We departed from thence keeping our course North East along the coaste, which wee founde more pleasant champion and without woods, with high mountaines within the lande continuing directly along the coast for the space of fiftie leagues, wee discouered 32. Ilelandes lying all neare the lande, being small and pleasant to the viewe, high and hauing many turnings and windings betwene them, making many fayre harboroughes and chanels as they doe in the goulfe of Venice in Saluonia, and Dalmatia, wee had no knowledge or acquaintance with the people: wee suppose they are of the same maners and nature that the others are. Sayling Northeast for the space of 150. leagues we approched

ched to the lande that in times past was discouered by the Britons, which is in fiftie degrees. Hauing now spent all our prouision and victuals, and hauing discouered about 700. leagues and more of newe Countries, and being furnished with Water and Wood wee concluded to returne into Fraunce.

Touching the religion of this people, which wee haue founde for want of their language we could not vnderstand neither by signes nor gesture that they had any religion or lawe at all, or that they did acknowledge any first cause or mouer, neither that they worship the heauen or starres the Sunne or Moone or other Planets, and much lesse whether they bee idolaters, neither coulde wee learne whether that they vsed any kinde of Sacrifices or other adorations, neither in their villages haue they any Temples or houses of prayer. We suppose that they haue no religion at all, and þ they liue at their owne libertie. And þ all this proceedeth of ignorance, for that they are very easie to bee persuaded: and all that they see vs Christians doe in our diuine seruice they did the same with the like imitation as they sawe vs to doe it.

B 4   The

❧ *The diſcouerie of the Iſles of Friſ-*
land, Iſeland, Engroueland, Eſtotiland, Drogeo and
Icaria, made by M. Nicolas Zeno, Knight, and M. An-
tonio his brother.

Jn the yere of our Lord 1200.
There was in the Citie of Venice a famous Gentleman, named M. Marino Zeno, who for
his great vertue and ſingular
wiſedome, was called and elec-
ted gouernour in certain common wealthes of Italy, in the
adminiſtration whereof hee
bore himſelfe ſo diſcreetly, that
hee was beloued of all men, and his name greatly reueren-
ced of thoſe that neuer knewe or ſawe his perſon. And a-
mong ſundrie his worthie workes, this is recorded of him,
that hee pacified certaine greeuous ciuile diſſentions that
aroſe among the Cittzens of Verona: whereas otherwiſe if
by his graue aduiſe and great diligence, they had not beene
preuented, the matter was likely to breake out in hot broiles
Podeſta. of warre. Hee was the firſt Agent that the common wealth
of Venice kept in Conſtantinople in the yeere 1205. *quan-*
do n'era patrona, conli baroni frãceſi. This Gentleman
had a ſonne named M. Pietro, who was the father of the
Duke Rinieri, which Duke dying with out iſſue, made his
heyre M. Andrea, the ſonne af M. Marco his brother. This
M. Andrea was captaine generall and Procurator, a man
of great reputation for many rare partes, that were in him.
He had a ſonne M. Rinieri, a worthie Senatour and pru-
dent Councellour: Of whom deſcende M. Pietro Generall of the league of the Chriſtians againſt the Turkes, who
was called Dragon , for that in his armes hee bare a
Dragon. Hee was father to M. Carlo the famous
Procurator and Generall againſte the Genowayes in
thoſe

those cruel warres, when as almost all the chiefe princes
of Europe did oppugne and seek to ouerthrow our Empire
and libertie, where by his great valiancie and prowesse like
an other Furius Camillus, he deliuered his Countrie from
the present perill it was in, being readie to become a pray &
spoyle vnto the enemie, wherefore hee was afterwarde sur-
named, the Lion, and for an eternall remembrance of his for-
situde and valiant exploits he gaue the Lion in his armes.
M. Carlo had two brethren, M. Nicolo, the knight & Antonio, the father M. Dragon, of whom issued M. Caterino, the
father of M. Pietro, this M. Pietro had sonnes M. Caterino, that dyed the last yeere, M. Francisco, M. Carlo, M.
Battista, and M. Vincenzo. That M. Caterino was father to
M. Nicolo, that is yet liuing. Now M. Nicolo, the knight,
being a man of great courage and very nobly minded, after
this foresaide warre of Genoua, that troubled so our prede-
cessours, entred into a wonderfull great desire and fansie to
see the fashions of the world, and to trauaile, and to acquaint
himselfe with the manners of sundry nations & learne their
languages, wherby afterwards vpō occasions hee might be
ye better able to do seruice to his coūtrie & purchase to himselfe credite & honor. Wherfore hee caused a shippe to bee
made & hauing furnished her at his proper charges (as hee
was very wealthie) hee departed out of our Seas & passing
the straites of Gibralterra, he sailed for certaine dayes vpon
ye Ocean keeping his course stil to ye Northwards, wt intent
to see England and Flaunders. Where being assaulted in
those Seas by a terrible tempest, was so tossed for the space
of many dayes with the Sea and winde that hee knewe not
where hee was, till at length hee discouered lande, and not
beeing able any longer to sustaine the violence of the tempest the ship was cast away vpon the Isle of Friseland. The
men were saued, and most part of the goods that were in the
Ship. And this was in the yeere 1380. The inhabitants
of the Iland came running in great multitudes wt weapons
to set vpon M. Nicolo and his men, who beeing sore wether
beaten and ouerlaboured at Sea, and not knowing in what

The ship of M.
N. Zeno cast a-
way vpon Frist-
land in anno.
1380.

C   pars

part of the worlde they were, were not able to make any resiſtaunce at all, much leſſe to defende them ſelues couragiouſly, as it behooued them in ſuch dangerous caſe. And they ſhoulde haue beene doubtleſſe very diſcourteouſly entreated and cruelly handeled, if by good hap there had not been hard by the place a Prince with armed people. Who vnderſtanding, that there was euen at that preſent a great ſhip caſt away vpon the Iland, came running at the noyſe and outcries that they made againſt our poore Mariners, and driuing away the inhabitants, ſpake in latine and aſked them what they were and from whence they came, and perceiuing ỹ they were Italians, ε all of one Countrie, he was ſurpriſed with marueilous great ioy . . Wherefore promiſing thẽall, that they ſhoulde receiue no diſcourteſie, and that they were come into a place where they ſhoulde bee well vſed and very welcome, he tooke them into his protection vpon his faith. This was a great Lord and poſſeſſed certaine Ilands called Porland, lying one the Southſide of Friſland being ỹ richeſt and moſt populous of all thoſe partes , his name was Zichmni: ε beſide the ſaid little Ilands, he was Duke of Sorani, lying within the land towards Scotland. Of theſe North partes I thought good to draw the copie of a Sea carde, which amongeſt other antiquities, I haue in my houſe, which although it be rotten through many yeres: yet it falleth out indifferent well, and to thoſe that are delighted in theſe things, it may ſerue for ſome light to the vnderſtanding of that, which without it cannot ſo eaſily be conceiued. Zichmni being Lorde of thoſe Seignories (as is ſaid) was a very warlike and valiant man ε aboue al things famous in Sea cauſes. And hauing this yeere before giuen the ouerthrowe to the king of Norway, who was Lord of the Ilande, beeing deſirous to winne fame by feates of armes, was come on land with his mẽ to giue the attẽpt, for ỹ winning of Friſland, which is an Iland much bigger then Ireland. Wherefore ſeeing that M. Nicolo was a mã of iudgement and diſcretion, and very expert both in Sea matters and martiall affaires, hee gaue him commiſſion to goe abord his nauie with all his men, charging the captaine to

A forraine prince hapning to be in Friſlãd w armed men. When M. Zeno ſuffered ſhipwrack, there came vnto him and ſpake latin.

Zichmni prince of Porland or Duke of Sorani.

Friſland the king of Norwayes.

honour him and in all things to vse his counsaile. This Nauie of Zichmni was of thirteene vessels, wherof two onely were with oares, the rest small barkes, and one ship, with the which they sayled to the Westwardes and with little paines wonne Ledouo and Ilofe and diuers other small Ilandes, and turning into a bay called Sudero, in the hauen of the towne named Sanestol they tooke certaine small Barks laden with salt fish. And heere they founde Zichmni, who came by land with his armie conquering all the countrie as he went, they staied here but a while but held on their course to the Westwards till they came to the other Cape of the goulfe or bay, then turning againe they found certaine Ilelandes and broken landes which they reduced all vnto the Seignorie and possession of Zichmni. These Seas for as much as they sayled, were in maner nothing but sholds and rocks, in sort that if M. Nicolo and the venetian mariners had not beene their Pilots, the whole Fleete in iudgement of all that were in it, had been cast away, so small was ye skill of Zichmnis men in respect of ours, who had been trained vp in the art and practise of nauigation all the daies of their life. Now the Fleete hauing doone such things, (as is declared) ye Captaine by the counsel of M. Nicolo, determined to goe a lande at a towne called Bondendon, to vnderstande what successe Zichmni had in his warres, where they heard to their great content, that he had fought a great battaile and put to flight the armie of his enemie: by reason of which victorie they sent Embassadours from all partes of the Ilande to yeeld the countrie vp into his handes, taking down their enseignes in euery towne and castell: They thought good to stay in that place for his comming, being reported for certaine that he would bee there very shortly. At his comming there was great congratulatiō and many signes of gladnes shewed, as wel for the victorie by lande as for that by Sea, for the which the venetians were honoured & extolled of all men, in such sort ye there was no talke but of them, and of ye great valour of M. Nicolo. Wherfore the Prince who was a great fauourer of valiant men and especially of those that

coulde

could behaue them ſelues well at the Sea, cauſed M. Nicolo to bee brought before him, and after hauing commended
him with many honourable ſpeeches, and prayſed his great
induſtrie and dexterie of wit, by the which, he acknowledged
himſelfe to haue receiued an ineſtimable benefite as the ſa-
uing of his Fleete and the winning of many places, he made
him Knight, and rewarded his men with many riche and
bountifull giftes : Then departing from thence they went
in triumphing maner towardes Frieſland, the chief Citie of
ỹ Iſlande, ſituate on the Southeſt ſide of the Iſle, within a
goulf, (as there are very many in that Iland). In this goulfe
or bay there is ſuch great abundance of fiſh taken, that many
ſhips are laden therewith to ſerue Flaunders, Britaine, England, Scotland, Norway and Denmarke, and by this trade
they gather great wealth.

And thus much is taken out of a letter, that M. Nicolo
ſent vnto M. Antonio his brother, requeſting him that hee
woulde ſeeke ſome meanes to come to him. Wherefore
hee, who had as great deſire to trauaile as his brother,
bought a Ship, and directing his courſe that way, after hee
had ſayled a great while and eſcaped many dangers, hee arriued at length in ſafetie with M. Nicolo, who receiued him
very ioyfully, for that hee was his brother not only in fleſhe
and blood, but alſo in valour and good qualities. M. Antonio remained in Frieſlande and dwelt there for the ſpace
of fourteene yeeres, foure yeeres with M. Nicolo, and ten
yeeres alone. Where they came into ſuch grace and fauour with the Prince, that hee made M. Nicolo, Captaine
of his Nauie, & with great preparation of warre they were
ſent foorth for the enterpriſe of Eſtlande, which lyeth vpon
the coaſte betweene Frieſland and Norway, where they did
many dōmages, but hearing that the king of Norway was
comming towardes them with a great Fleet, they departed
wt ſuch a terrible flaw of wind ỹ they were driue vpō certain
ſholdes. Where a great part of their ſhips were caſt away, ỹ
reſt were ſaued vpō Griſland, a great Iland but diſhabited.

The

M. Zeno, made
knight by
Zichmni.

Ships laden
with fiſh at fric-
land: for Flaun-
ders, Britaine.
England, Scot
land, Norway,
and Denmark.
But not to bee
proued that euer
any came thēce.
A letter ſent by
maſter. N. Zeno
from Frieſland
to his brother,
M. Antonio in
Uenice.
End of the firſt
letter.

The king of Norway his fleete being taken with the same
storme, did vtterly perishe in those seas. Whereof Zichmni
hauing notice, by a shippe of his enemies, that was cast by
chaunce vpon Grisland. Hauing repayred his fleete, and
perceyuing him selfe northerly neere vnto the Islandes, determined to set vpon Islande, which together with the rest
was subiect to the king of Norway: But he founde the countrey so well fortified and defended, that his fleete beeing so
small and very ill appointed both of weapons and men, hee
was gladde to retire. And so hee left that enterprise without perfourming any thing at all, and in the same chanelles
he assaulted the other Iles called the Islands, which are seuen
Talas, Broas, Iscant, Trans, Mimant, Dambere, & Bres,
and hauing spoyled them all, hee built a fort in Bres, where
he left M. Nicolo, with certaine small barkes and men and
munition. And nowe thinking he had done well for this voyage, with those fewe shippes which were left hee returned
into Frieslande. M. Nicolo remayning nowe in Bres determined vpon a time to goe forth and discouer lande, wherefore arming out their small barkes in the moneth of Iuly, he
sayled to the Northwardes, and arriued in Engrouelande.
Where he founde a monastery of Fryers of the order of the
Predicators, and a Church dedicated to S. Thomas harde
by a hill, that casteth forth fire, like Vesuuius and Etna.
There is a fountayne of hot burning water with the whiche
they heate the Churche of the monasterie and the Fryers
chambers, it commeth also into the kitchen so boyling hotte,
that they vse no other fire to dresse their meate, and putting
their bread into brasse pottes without any water, it doeth
bake as it were in a hot ouen. They haue also small gardens, couered ouer in the winter time, which being watered
with this water are defended from the force of the snowe
and colde, which in those parts being situate farre vnder the
pole, is very extreeme; and by this meanes they produce flowers and fruites and herbes of sundrie sortes, euen as in o-
ther temperate countreys in their seasons in suche sorte that
the rude and sauage people of those partes seeing these su-

(marginal notes:) Engrouelande. Preaching Friers of S. Thomas.

A notable hea-

C 3   pernaturall

pernaturall effectes doe take those Friers for Gods, and
bring them many presentes as chickens, fleshe and diuers o-
ther thinges, and haue them all in great reuerence as Lords.
When the frost and snowe is great, they heate their houses
in maner before said, and will by letting in the water or opening the windowes, temper the heate and colde at their pleasure. In y buildings of the monastery they vse no other matter but that which is ministred vnto them by the fire, for they
take the burning stones, that are cast out as it were sparkles
or ceindres at the firie mouth of the hill, and when they are
most enflamed, cast water vpon them, wherby they are dissol-
ued and become excellēt white lime and so tough that being
contriued in building it lasteth for euer. And the very sparkles after the fire is out of them do serue in steede of stones to
make walles and vautes: for being once colde they will neuer dissolue or breake except they be cut with some irō toole,
and the vautes that are made of them are so light that they
need no sustentacle or proppe to holde them vp, and they wil
endure continually very fayre and whole. By reason of these
great commodities the friers haue made there so many buildings and walles, that it is a wonder to see. The couerts or
roofes of their houses for the most part are made in this maner, first they rayse the wall vp to his full height, then they
make it enclining or bowing in by litle and litle in forme of
a vaute. But they are not greatly troubled with raine in
those partes, for that, by reason of the pole or colde climate,
the first snowe being falne it thaweth no more for the space of
nine moneths, for so long dureth their winter. They feede
of the fleshe of wilde beastes & of fish, for where as the warme
water falleth into the sea, there is a large and wide hauen,
which by reason of the heate of the water, doeth neuer freeze
all the winter, by meanes whereof there is suche concourse
and flocks of sea foule and such aboundance of fishe, that they
take thereof infinite multitudes, whereby they maintayne a
great number of people rounde about whiche they keepe in
continuale worke, both in building and taking of foules and
fishe, and in a thousande other necessarie affaires and busines
about

about the monasterie.

Their houses are builte about the hill on euery side, in fourme rounde, and 25. foote broade, and in mounting vpwardes they goe narower and narower, leauing at the toppe a litle hole, whereat the ayre commeth in, to giue light to the house, and the flore of the house is so hot, that being within they feele no colde at all. Hither in the sommer time come many barkes from the Ilands there about, & from the Cape aboue Norway and from Trondon. And bring to the Friers al maner things that may be desired, taking in change thereof fishe which they drie in the sunne or in the colde, and skins of diuers kindes of beastes. For the which they haue wood to burne and timber verie artificially carued, and corne & cloth to make them apparell. For in change of the two foresayde commodities all the nations bordering rounde about them couet to trafficke with them, and so they without any trauell or expences haue that which they desire. To this monasterie resort Friers of Norway, of Suetia and of other countreys but the most part are of the Islandes. There are continually in that part many barkes, whiche are kept in there by reason of the sea being frozen, wayting for the season of the yeere to dissolue the Ice. The fishers boates are made like vnto a weuers shuttle, taking the skins of fishes, they fashió them with the bones of the same fishes, and sowing thé together in many doubles they make them so sure and substanciall, that it is miraculous to see, how in tempests they will shut théselues close within, and let the sea and winde carrie them, they care not whether, without any feare eyther of breaking or drowning. And if they chance to be driuen vpó any rocks, they remaine sounde, without the least bruse in the worlde: And they haue as it were a sleeue in the bottome which is tied fast in ÿ middle, & when there cómeth any water into their boat, they put it into the one halfe of ÿ sleeue, thé fastning ÿ ende of it wt two peeces of wood and loosing ÿ band beneath they conuey the water forth of the boate: and this they doe as often as they haue occasion without any perill or impediment at all. Moreouer, the water of the monasterie being of sulphurious

Trade in sommer time from Trondon to S. Thomas friers in Ingroucláu.

Resort of friers from Norway & Sueden, to the monasterie in Ingrouelande called S. Ths.

of brimstone nature is conueyed into the lodginges of the principall Friers by certaine vessels of brasse, tinne or stone so hotte that it heateth the place as it were a stowe, not carrying with it any stinke or other noysome smell.

Besides this they haue another conueyance to bring hot water with a wall vnder the ground to the ende it should not freese, vnto the middle of the court, where it falleth into a great vessel of brasse, that standeth in the middle of a boyling fountayne, and this is to heate their water to drinke and to water their gardens, and thus they haue from the hill the greatest commodities that may be wished, and so these Fryers employ all their trauaile and studie for the most part in trimming their gardins and in making faire and beawtifull buildings and especially handsome and commodious, neyther are they destitute of ingenious and painefull artificers for the purpose, for they giue very large payment, and to them that bring them fruites and seedes they are very bountifull and giue they care not what. So that there is great resort of workemen and maisters in diuers faculties, by reason of the good gaines and large allowance that is there.

In the monasterie S. Thomas most of them speake the latin tongue, and of the two letter.

The most of them speake the Latin tongue, and especially the superiours and principalls of the monasterie. And this is as muche as is knowen of Engrouelande, which is all by the relation of M. Nicolo, who maketh also particular description of a riuer, that he discouered, as is to be seene in the carde that I drewe. And in the ende M. Nicolo not being vsed and acquainted with these cruell coldes, fell sicke, and a litle while after returned into Frislande, where he dyed. He left behinde him in Venice two sonnes, M. Giouanni and M. Toma, who had two sonnes M. Nicolo, the father of the famous Cardinal Zeno, and M. Pietro of whom descended the other Zenos, that are liuing at this day.

M. Zeno died in Frislande.

Now M. Nicolo being dead, M. Aotonio succeeded him both in his goods and in his dignities & honour, and albeit he attempted diuers wayes and made greate supplication hee coulde neuer obtaine licence to returne into his Countrey. For Zichmni had determined to make himselfe Lorde of

the

the sea.   Wherefore vsing alwayes the counsaile and seruice of M. Antonio, hee sent hym with some small barkes to the Westwardes, for that towardes those partes some of his fishermen had discouered certaine Ilandes verye rich and populous, whiche discouerie, M. Antonio in a letter to his brother M. Carlo, recounteth from point to point in this manner , sauing that wee haue chaunged some olde woordes , leauing the matter entire as it was

Sixe and twentie yeeres agoe there departed foure Fisher boates, the whiche a mightie tempest arising, were tossed for the space of manye dayes verye desperately vpon the Sea, when at length the tempeste ceassyng and the weather waxing fayre they discouered an Ilande called Estotilande, lying to the Westwardes aboue 1000. Miles from Frislande, vpon the whiche one of the boates was caste awaye, and sixe men that were in it were taken of the inhabitauntes and brought vnto a verye fayre and populous Citie , where the kyng of the place sent for manye interpreters , but there was none coulde bee founde that vnderstoode the language of the fishermen , excepte one that spake Latin, who was also cast by chaunce vpon the same Ilande, who in the behalfe of the kyng asked them what Countreymen they were , and so vnderstanding theyr case , rehearsed it vnto the King, who willed that they shoulde tarrie in the Countrey , wherefore they obeyinge his commaundement for that they coulde not otherwise doe, dwelte fiue yeeres in the Ilande , and learned the language, and one of them was in diuers partes of the Ilande, and reporteth that it is a verye riche Countrey , abounding with all the commodities of the worlde, and that it is little lesse than Islande , but farre more fruitesull, hauing in the middle thereof a verye hyghe mountayne, from the whiche there riseth foure Riuers, that passe throughe the whole Countrey.

The inhabitantes are very wittie peeple , and haue all the artes and faculties as wee haue : and it is credible, that in time past they haue had trafficke with our men , for he

saide

Marginal notes:

3. letter beginneth from the second brother M. Antonio out of Frislande, to his other brother in Uenice named Messer Carlo. Estotiland.

6. Fisher men taken.

Fishermen of Frislande spake latin.

Sixe were 5. yeeres in Estotilande.

One of the fisfiers of Frisland reporteth of Estotilande. Estotilande riche abounding with al the commodit of the worlde.

sayde that he sawe latin bookes in the Kings library, whiche they at this present doe not vnderstande, they haue a peculiar language and letters or caracters to them selues. They haue mines of all manner of mettals, but especially they abounde with golde. They haue their trade in Engroueland from whence they bring skins and brimstone and pitch: And he saith that to ý southwards, there is a great populous coūtrey very rich of gold. They sowe corne and make bere or ale, which is a kind of drinke that the north people doe vse as we do wine. They haue mightie great woods, they make their buildings with wals, and there are many cities & castels. They build smal barkes and haue sayling, but they haue not the lodestone nor know not the vse of the cōpasse. Wherfore these fishers were had in great estimatiō, insomuch that the king sent them with 12. barkes to the southwardes to a countrey whiche they call Drogio: but in their voyage they had suche countrary weather, that they thought all to haue perished in the sea, but yet escaping that cruell death, they fel into another more cruel. For they were takē in the countrey and the most parte of them eaten by the Sauage people, which feede vpon mans fleshe, as the sweetest meate in their iudgementes that is.

But that fisher with his fellowes shewyng them the maner of taking fishe with nettes, saued their liues: and woulde goe euery day a fishing to the sea and in fresh riuers, and take great aboundance of fish and giue it to the chiefe men of the countrey, whereby hee got him selfe so great fauour, that hee was very well beloued and honoured of euery one.

The fame of this man being spred abroad in the countrey, there was a Lorde thereby that was verie desirous to haue him with him, and to see howe hee vsed his miraculous arte of catching fishe, in so muche that he made warre with the other Lorde, with whom hee was before, and in the ende preuayling, for that hee was more mightie and a better warriour, the fisherman was sent vnto him with the rest of his company. And for the space of thirteene yeeres that hee dwelt in those partes, he saith, that he was sent in this order

to

Aboundance of golde.

trade from Estotiland, to Engroueland skins, brimstone and pitche.

Gold, corne, and bere, or ale.

Many cities and castles.

A countrey called Drogio.

The 6. fishermē of Frisland only saued, by shewing the maner to take fishe.

The chiefest of the 6. fishers, specified before & his cōpanions

In the space of 13. yeres in Drogio.

so more than 25. Lordes, for they had continuall warre a-mongest them selues, this Lorde with that Lord and he with an other, onely to haue him to dwell with them, so that wan-dring vp and downe the Countrey without any certayne a-bode in one place, hee knewe almost all those partes. He saith that it is a very great countrey and as it were a newe world, the people very rude and voyde of all goodnesse, they goe all naked so that they are miserablie vexed with colde, neyther haue they the wit to couer their bodies with beastsskins, which they take in huntinge, they haue no kind of metal, they liue by hun-ting, they carie certain lances of wood, made sharp at the point, they haue bowes, the stringes whereof are made of beastes skinnes : They are a very fierce people, they make cruell warres one with another, and eate one an other, they haue gouernours and certayne lawes verye diuers amongest them selues. But the farther to the South westwardes, the more ciuility there is, the ayre being somewhat temperat, so that there they haue Cities, and temples to Idolls, where-in they sacrifice men and afterwardes eate them, they haue there some knowledge and vse of gold and siluer.

Nowe this fisher hauing dwelt so many yeeres in those countreys, purposed if it were possible to returne home in-to his countrey, but his companions dispayring euer to see it agayne, let him goe in Gods name, they kept them selues, where they were. Wherefore hee bidding them farewel, fledde through the woods towardes Drogio, and was verie well receiued of the Lorde that dwelt next to that place who knewe him and was a great enemie of the other Lorde, and so running from one Lorde to an other, being those by whom hee had passed before, after long time and many trauelles he came at length to Drogio where hee dwelt three yeeres. When as by good fortune he heard by the inhabitants, that there were certaine boates arriued vpon the coast, wherfore entring into good hope to accomplish his intent, he went to the sea side & asking them of what countrey they were, they answered of Es-totiland whereat he was exceeding glad, and requested that

Sent to more then 25. lords, which continually war-red amongst the selues for the same fisherman.

3. yeres in Dro-gio.

Where by happ arriu. d certaine boates from: E-stotiland.

they

he became interpreter for ye men that ariued at Drozeo in the boates of Esto-tilande.

Afterwards hee frequ nted that trade with them in such sort, that he became very rich. And so fur-nished a bark of his owne & re-turned to Fris-lande where hee reported the sto-ry to his Lorde Zichmni.

Zichmni minded to send M. An-tonio Zeno with a fleete towards those partes of Estotilande, and of 3 letter.

4. letter be-ginneth frō M. Antonio in Esto-tiland, to his bro-ther Carlo in Uenice.
The fisherman dead that should haue bin guid & interpreter.
Certaine mar-riners taken in his steede which came with him frō Estotiland. July. Ile Ilofe.

they woulde take him into them, whiche they did verye willingly, and for that hee had the language of the Countrey and there was none of them coulde speake it they vsed him for their interpreter.

And after that hee frequented that trade with them, in such sorte that hee became verye riche and so furnishing out a barke of his owne hee returned into Frislande, where hee made reporte vnto this Lorde of that welthie Countrey. And hee is throughly credited because of the Mariners, who approoue many straunge thinges, that hee reporteth to bee true. Wherefore this Lorde is resolued to sende me foorth with a fleete towardes those partes, and there are so manye that desire to goe in the voyage, for the noueltie and strange-nesse of the thing, that I thinke we shall be very strongly ap-pointed, without any publike expence at all. And this is the tenor of the letter before mentioned which I haue heere set downe, to giue intelligence of an other voyage, that M. An-tonio made, being set out with many Barkes and men, not-withstanding hee was not captaine as hee had thought at the first hee shoulde, for Zichmni went in his owne person: & concerning this matter I haue a letter in forme as folow-eth. Our great preparation for the voyag of Estotiland, was begun in an vnluckie houre, for three dayes before our de-parture, the fisherman died, that shoulde haue been our guid: notwithstanding this Lorde woulde not giue ouer the enter-prize, but in steade of the fisherman tooke certayne Marri-ners that returned out of the Ilande with him, and so ma-king our nautgation to the Westwards, we discouered cer-tayne Ilandes subiect to Frislande, and hauing passed cer-tayne shelues we stayed at Ledouo for the space of 7. dayes to refreshe our selues, and furnish the fleete with necessarie prouision. Departing from hence we arriued the first of Ju-ly at the Ile of Ilofe, and for that the winde made for vs, wee stayed not there, but passed foorth, & being vpon the maine sea, there arose immediatly a cruell tempest wherewith for eight dayes space wee were miserably vexed, not knowing where wee were, and a great part of the Barkes were

were cast away, afterwarde waxing faire wether we gathered vp the broken peeces of the Barkes that were lost, and
sayling with a prosperous winde wee discouered lande at
West.   Wherefore keeping our course directly vpon it,
wee arriued in a very good and safe harborough, where wee
sawe an infinite companie of people readie in armes, come
running very furiously to the water side, as it were for de-
fence of the Ilande .   Wherefore Zichimni causing his
men to make signes of peace vnto them, they sent tenne men
vnto vs that coulde speake tenne languages, but wee coulde
vnderstande none of them, except one that was of Island. He
being brought before our Prince and asked, what was the
name of the Iland, and what people inhabited it, and who
gouerned it, answered, that the Iland was called Icaria, and
that all the kinges that had raigned there, were called Icari,
after the name of the first king of that place, which as they
say was the sonne of Dedalus king of Scotland, who conquering that Iland, left his sonne there for king, and left them
those lawes that they retaine to this present, and after this, he
desiring to sayle further, in a great tempest that arose, was
drowned, wherefore for a memoriall of his death, they call
those Seas yet, the Icarian Sea, and the kings of the Iland
Icari, and for that they were contented with that state, which
god had giue them, neither wholp they alter one iote of their
lawes and customes, they would not receiue any straunger,
wherefore they requested our Prince, that hee woulde not
seeke to violate their lawes, which they had receiued from
that king of worthie memorie and obserued very duly to that
present: which if hee did attempt, it woulde redounde to his
manifest destruction, they being all resolutely bent rather to
leaue their life, than to loose in any respect the vse of their
lawes.   Notwithstanding, that wee should not thinke they
did altogether refuse the conuersation and trafficke with
other men, they tolde vs for conclusion that they would willingly receiue one of our men, and preferre him to be one
of y chiefe amongest them, only to learne my language the
Italian tongue, and to bee enformed of our maners and cu-

D 3   stomes,

Zichmni his first Discouery of the Iland Icaria.

Infinit number of people in armes.

An Island man in Icaria.

Icaria Ilande. All the kings y had raigned in that Ilad were called Icari after the name of the first king of y place: which they say was the sonne of Deda- lus king of Scots. Icarius drow- ned. Icarian Sea.

The people of Icaria destrous of the Italian tongue.

Hauing in that Iland 10. men of ten sundry nations.

stomes, as they had alreadie receiued those other tenne of tenne sundrie nations, that came vnto their Iland. To these things our Prince answered nothing at all, but causing his men to seeke some good harborough, hee made signes as though he would come on land, and sayling round about the Iland, hee espied at length a harborough on the East side of the Ilande, where he put in with all his Fleet, the mariners went on land to take in wood and water, which they did with as great speede as they coulde, doubting least they shoulde be assaulted by the inhabitants as it fell out in deed, for those that dwelt there abouts, making signes vnto the other with fire and smoke, put them selues presently in armes and the other comming to them, they came al running downe to the Sea side vpon our men, with bowes and arrowes and other weapons, that many were slaine and diuers sore wounded. And we made signes of peace vnto them, but it was to no purpose, for their rage encreased more and more, as though they had fought for life and liuing. Wherefore wee were forced to depart and to sayle along in a great circuite about the Iland, being alwaies accompanied vpon the hil tops and

Infinite multitude of armed men in Icaria.

the Sea coast with an infinite multitude of armed men, and so doubling the Cape of the Iland towardes the North, wee found many great sholdes amongst the which for the space of ten daies we were in continual danger of loosing our whole Fleete, but that it pleased God all that while to send vs very faire weather. Wherefore proceeding on till we came to ye East cape, we sawe the inhabitaunts still on the hill tops & by the Sea coast keepe with vs, and in making great outcries & shooting at vs a farre of they vttered their olde spitefull affection towards vs. Wherefore we determined to stay in some safe harborough, and see if we might speak once againe with the Islander, but our determination was frustrate, for the people more like vnto beastes than men, stood continually in armes wt intent to beat vs backe, if we shoulde come on lande. Wherefore Zichmni seeing hee coulde not preuaile and thought if hee shoulde haue perseuered and

followed

followed obstinately his purpose, their victuals would haue failed them, hee departed with a faire winde and sailed sixe dayes to the Westwards, but the winde chaunging to the Southwest and the Sea waxing rough wee sayled 4. dayes with the wind in the powpe and at length discouering land, wee were afraide to approch neere vnto it, being the Sea growen, and we not knowing what lande it was, but God prouided for vs, that the winde ceasing there came a greate calme. Wherefore some of our companie rowing to land with oares, returned and brought vs word to our great comforte, that they had founde a very good Countrie and a better harborough, vpon which newes wee towed our ships & sinal Barkes to land, and being entred into the harborough, wee sawe a farre of a great mountaine, ý cast forth smoke, which gaue vs good hope that we shoulde finde some inhabitantes in ý Iland, neither would Zichmni rest, although it were a great way of, but send a 100. good souldiers to search the Countrie and bring report what people they were that inhabited it, and in the meane time they tooke in wood & water for the prouision of the Fleete, and catcht great store of fishe and Sea foule and founde such abundance of birdes egges that our men that were halfe famished, were filled withall. Whiles we were riding here, began the moneth of June, at which time the ayre in the Iland was so temperate and pleasant as is impossible to expresse, but when we coulde see no people at all, wee suspected greatly that this pleasant place was desolate and dishabited. Wee gaue name to the hauen calling it Trim, and the point that stretched out into ý sea wee called Capo di Trim. The 100. souldiers that were sent foorth, eight dayes after returned, and brought worde that they had been through the Ilande and at the mountaine and that the smoke was a naturall thing proceeding from a great fire that was in the bottome of the hill, and that there was a spring from which issued, a certaine matter like pitch, which ran into the Sea, and that there aboutes dwelt greate multitudes of people half wilde, hiding theselues in caues of

Zichmni departed from Icari Westwards.

Sight of land.

100. good souldiers sent by Zichmni to learch the countrie (which countrie is not named.)

June.
The ayre so temperate & sweete, as impossible to expresse it.

Hauen Trim.

Capo di Trim.
The 100. souldiers returned which had been through the Iland, report what they sawe and found.

the

the grounde, of fmall ftature, and very fearefull, for as foone as they fawe them they fled into their holes, and that there was a great riuer and a very good harborough. Zichmni being thus enformed, and feeing that it had a holfome and pure ayre, and a very fruitefull foyle and fayre riuers with fundrie other commodities, fell into fuch liking of the place, that hee determined to inhabite it, and build there a Citie.

But his people being weary and faint with their long and tedious trauaile began to tumult and murmure, faying that they woulde returne into their Countrie, for that the winter was at hand, and if they entred into the harborough, they fhould not be able to come out againe before the next Sommer. Wherefore hee retaining only the Barkes with Oares and fuch as were willing to ftay with him, fent all the reft with the fhippes backe againe, and willed that I, (though vnwilling) fhould bee their Captaine. I therefore departing, fayled for the fpace of twentie dayes to the Eftwards without fight of any land, then turning up courfe towardes Southeaft in fiue dayes I difcouered lande and founde my felfe vpon the Ile of Neome and knowing the Countrie, I perceiued I was paft Iflande: wherefore taking in fome frefh victuals of the inhabitants being fubiect to Zichmni, I fayled with a faire winde in three dayes to Frifland, where the people, who thought they had loft their Prince, becaufe of his long abfence, in this our voyage, receiued vs very ioyfully.

What followed after this letter I know not but by coniecture, which I gather out of a peece of another letter, which I will fet downe heere vnderneath: That Zichmni builte a towne in the port of the Iland that hee difcouered, and that hee fearched the Countrie very diligently and difcouered it all, and alfo the riuers on both fides of Engroueland, for that I fee it particularly defcribed in the Sea card, but the difcourfe or narration is loft. The beginning of the letter is thus. Concerning thofe things that you defire to knowe of mee, as of the men and their manners and cuftomes, of the beaftes and the Countries adioyning, I haue

Zichmni determining to remaine in the new difcouered land, kept with him his barkes with oares, and mē that were willing & fent the reft away homewards: Appointing Antonio Zeno chiefe captaine of them.
Antonio Zeno had fight of Neome, and knewe himfelfe paft Ifland.
Ende of the 4. letter.
A peece of a 5. letter.

Beginning of the letter.

haue made thereof a particular booke, which by Gods helpe
I will bring with mee: Wherein I haue described the countrie, the monstrous fishes, ẙ customes and lawes of Frisland,
Island, Estland, the kingdome of Norway, Estotiland, Drogio, and in the ende the life of master Nicolo, the knight
our brother, with the discouerie which he made and of Gro-
land. I haue also written the life and acts of Zichmni, a
Prince as worthie of immortall memory, as any that euer
liued, for his great valiancie and singuler humanitie, wherein I haue described the discouerie of Engroueland on both
sides, and the Citie that hee builded. Therefore I will
speake no further hereof in this letter, hoping to be with you
very shortly, and to satisfie you in sundrie other thinges by
worde of mouth. All these letters were written by master
Antonio to master Carlo his brother. And it greeueth me,
that the booke and diuers other writinges concerning these
purposes, are miserably lost: For I beeing but a child, when
they came to my handes, and not knowing what they were,
(as the manner of children is) I tore them, and rent them in
peeces, which now I cannot call to remembrance but to my
greef. Notwithstanding, that the memory of so many good
thinges shoulde not bee lost: whatsoeuer I could get of this
matter, I haue disposed and put in order, in the former discourse, to the ende that this age might bee partly satisfi-
ed, to ẙ which wee are more beholden for the great discoueries made in those partes, then to any other of the time past,
beeing most studious of the relations of the discoueries of
strange Countries, made by the great mindes, and industry
of our auncetours.

This discourse was collected by *Ramusio* Secretarie to
the state of Venice, (or by the Printer Tho. Gi-
unti.)

Iohn Baptista Ramusio, died in **Padua**
in Iuly, 1557.

€

¶ The true and laſt diſcouerie of Florida made by Captaine Iohn Ribault in the yeere 1562. Dedicated to a great noble man of Fraunce, and tranſlated into Engliſhe by one Thomas Hackit.

Here as in the yeere of our Lorde God 1562. it pleaſed God to moue your honour, to chooſe and appoint vs, to diſcouer and view a certaine long coaſt of the Weſt India, from the head of the lande called Laflorida, drawing towarde the North part, vnto the head of Britons, diſtant from the ſaide head of Laflorida 900. leagues, or there about : to the ends wee might certifie you & make true report of the temperature, fertilitie, Portes, Hauens, Riuers, and generally of all the commodities that bee ſeene and found in that lande, and alſo to learne what people were there dwelling, which thing you haue long time agoe deſired, beeing ſtirred therevnto by this zeale: That Fraunce might one day through newe diſcoueries haue knowledge of ſtrange Countries, and alſo thereof to receiue (by meanes of continuall trafficke) riche and ineſtimable commodities, as other nations haue done by taking in hand ſuch farre nauigations, both to the honor and prowes of their kings and princes, & alſo to the encreaſe of great profite and vſe to their common wealthes, countries & dominions, which is moſt of all without compariſō to be conſidered & eſteemed. It ſeemeth well ý yee haue been ſtirred herevnto euen of God aboue, & led to it by the hope & deſire you haue that a number of brutiſhe people and ignorant of Ieſus Chriſte, may by his grace come to ſome knowledge of his holy Lawes and Ordinaunces. So therefore it ſeemeth that it hath pleaſed God by his godly prouidence to

reſerue

referue the care which hee hath had of their ſaluation vntill this time, and will bꝛing them to our faith, at the time by himſelfe alone foꝛeſeene and oꝛdeined. Foꝛ if it were needfull to ſhewe howe many from time to time haue gone about to finde out this great lande, and to inhabite there: who neuertheleſſe haue alwaies failed & beene put by from their intention and purpoſe: ſome by feare of ſhipwꝛackes, and ſome by great windes and tempeſtes that moue them backe to their merueilous griefe. Of the which there was one

Sebaſtian Gabota.

a very famous ſtranger named Sebaſtian Gabota an excellent Pylot ſent thither by king Henry, the yeere 1498. and many others, who neuer could attaine to any habitation noꝛ take poſſeſſion thereof one only foote of grounde, noꝛ yet apꝛoche oꝛ enter into theſe parttes and faire riuers into the which God hath bꝛought vs. Wherefoꝛe (my Loꝛde) it may bee well ſaide that the liuing God hath reſerued this great lande foꝛ your pooꝛe ſeruantes and ſubiectes, as well to the ende they might bee made great ouer this pooꝛe people, & rude nation: as alſo to appꝛoue the foꝛmer affection which our kings haue had vnto this diſcouerie.

Foꝛ ẏ late king Frances the firſt (of happie memoꝛie) a Pꝛince endued with excellent vertues. The yeere 1524. ſent a famous and notable man a Floꝛentine, named Maſter John Uerarzan, to ſearch and diſcouer the Weſt

John Uerarꝛã.

parts as farre as might be: Who departing from Deepe with two veſſels little differing from the making and burden of theſe two Pinnaces of the kinges, which your honour hath oꝛdeined foꝛ this pꝛeſent nauigation. In the which land they haue found the eleuation the Pole, an viii. degrees. The Countrie (as he wꝛiteth) goodly, fruitfull, and ſo good temperature, that it is not poſſible to haue a better: beeing then as yet of no mã ſeen, noꝛ diſcerned. But they being not able to bꝛing to paſſe at this firſt voyage that which he had inteuded, noꝛ to arriue in any Poꝛt, by reaſon of ſundꝛie incouuenienences (which cõmôly happẽ) were cõſtrained to return into Fraunce: where after his arriuall, he neuer ceaſſed to make

ſuice

suite vntill he was sent thither againe, where at last he died.
The which occasion gaue small courage to sende thither a-
gayne, and was the cause that this laudable enterprise was
left of, vntill the yeere 1534. at which time his Maiestie, (desiring alwayes to enlarge his kingdome, countreys and dominions, and the aduauncing and ease of his subiectes) sent
thither a Pilote of S. Mallowes, a briton, named James
Cartier, well seene in the art and knowledge of Nauigati-   **James Cartier**
on, & especially of the North parts, commonly called the new
land, led by some hope to find passage that waies to the south
seas : Who being not able at his first going to bring any
thing to passe, that he pretended to do: was sent thither againe
the yeere following, and likewise Le sire Hemerall, and as
it is well knowen they did inhabite and builde, and plant the
kings armies in the North part a good way in the lande, as
farre as Tauadu and Ochisaon . Wherefore (my Lord)
trust iustly that a thing so commendable and worthie to bee
with good courage attempted, that God woulde guid and
keepe vs, desiring alwayes to fulfill your commaundement.
When wee had done your businesse, and made our prepara-
tions the xviii. day of Februarie 1562 through the fauour of
God wee departed with our two vessels out of the hauen of
Claue de Grace into the road Caux: and the next day hoysted
vp saile (the winde being in ỹ East) which lasted so fiue daies,
that we coulde not arriue at the nauch that is from betweene
the coast of Briton and Englande and the Iles of Surlinos
and Wiskam : So that the Winde blowing with great fu-
ry and tempest out of the West, and West Southwest, altogether contrary to our way and course, and all that we could
doe was to none effecte, besides the great daunger of breaking of our Mastes , as also to be hindered in our other labours. Wherefore as well to shonne many other inconueniences, which might follow to the preiudice and breach of our
voyage, hauing regard also to the likely daunger of death, ỹ
some of our gentlemen and souldiers being troubled with
feuers and whot sicknesses, might haue fallen into : as also

foȝ other conſiderations,wee thought good to fall into the
road of Breſt in Britaine,to ſet there our ſick folke on land,
and ſuffer the tempeſt to paſſe .   From whence (after wee
had taried there two dayes) wee returned againe to Sea-
warde to followe our nauigation,ſo that (my Loȝde) albeit
the winde was foȝ a long ſeaſon very much againſt vs, and
troubleſome : yet at the ende (God giuing vs thȝough his
grace and accuſtomed goodneſſe a meetely fauourable
winde) J determined with all diligence to pȝoue a newe
courſe which hath not beene yet attempted : trauerſing the
Seas of Oction 1800. Leagues at the leaſt, whiche in
deed is the true and ſhoȝt courſe that hereafter muſt be kept,
to the honour of our nation,reiecting the old conſerued opi-
on,which to long time hath beene holden as true.

     Which is, as it was thought a thing impoſſible to haue
the winde at Eaſt,Noȝtheaſt,and keepe the race and courſe
wee enterpȝiſed,but that we ſhoulde be dȝiuen towarde the
regi on of Affrica,the Jles of Canaria, Madera, and other
landes there aboutes. And the cauſe why we haue beene the
moȝe pȝouoked and aſſured to take this newe race,hath bin becauſe that it ſeemed to euery one,that we might not paſſe noȝ
goe in this Nauigation without the ſight and touching of
the Antillies and Lucaries,and there ſoiourne and take freſh
waters and other neceſſaries, as the Spaniards doe in their
voyage to new ſpaine:wherof(thanked be God)we haue had
no neede,noȝ entered the chanell of Roham : which hath bin
thought impoſſible. Foȝeſeeing alſo that it was not expedient
foȝ vs to paſſe thȝough the Jlandes,as wel to ſhune many inconueniences that might happen in paſſing that way(wherof
ſpȝingeth nothing but innumerable quarrels,pleadings, cõ-
fuſions,and bȝeach of al woȝthy enterpȝiſes,and goodly nauigations,whereof enſueth complaintes and odious queſtions
betweene the ſubiectes of the king and his friends and alies)
as alſo to the ende they might vnderſtand,that in the time to
come(God hauing ſhewed vs ſuch graces, as theſe his wonderfull benefites firſte ſhewed to the pooȝe people of this ſo
                                                              goodly

goodly newe framing people, of so gentle a nature, and a
countrey so pleasant and fruitefull, lacking nothing at all
that may seeme necessarie for mans food)we would not haue
to doe with their Ilandes,and other landes: which (for that
they first discouered them) they keepe with much ielousie :
trusting that if God will suffer the king (through your per-
swation) to cause some part of this incomparable countrey
to be peopled and inhabited with such a number of his poore
subiectes as you shall thinke good, there neuer happened in
the memory of man so great and good commoditie to France
as this,and (my Lorde)for many causes, whereof a man is
neuer able to say or write to the ful,as vnder the assured hope
that we haue alwayes had in executing vprightly that which
I had receiued in charge of you, God woulde blesse our
wayes and nauigations. After we had constantly and with
diligence in time conuenient determined vpon the way,wee
shoulde haue thought it noysome and tedious to all our companie, if it had before bin knowe vnto any without tourning
or wauering to or fro from their first ententio. And notwithstanding that satan did often what he could to sowe many ob-
stractes,troubles and lettes, according to his acustomed sub-
tilties,so it is come to passe, that God by his onely goodnes
hath giuen vs grace,to make the furthest arte and trauars of
the seas,that euer was made in our memorie or knowledge,
in longitude from the East to the West:and therefore was it
commonly sayde both in Fraunce and Spaine, and also a-
mong vs,that it was impossible for vs safely to ariue thither,
whither the Lord did conduct vs:Al which perswaded but of
igoraunce and lacke of attempting:which wee haue not bin
afrayde to giue aduenture to prooue. Albeit that all Mariners Cardes doe set the Coastes with shipwrackes without portes or Riuers : which wee haue found otherwise as it
followeth.

    Thursday the last of Aprill at the breake of the day ,
wee discouered and clearely perceyued a fayre Coast,stret-
chyng of a great length couered with an infinite number of
high

high and fayre trees, wee being not paſt 7. oꝛ 8. leagues from the ſhoꝛe, the countrey ſeeming vnto vs plaine without anye ſhewe of hils, and appꝛoching neerer within foure oꝛ fiue leagues of the land, we caſt an ancker at ten fadome water, the bottome of the Sea being plaine with muche Oꝛias and faſt holde on the South ſide, as farre as a certaine point oꝛ Cape ſituate vnder that Latitude of nine and twentie degrees and a halfe, which we haue named Cape Francois.

Wee coulde eſpie neither Riuer noꝛ Bay, wherefoꝛe wee ſent our Boates furniſhed with men of experience, to ſounde and knowe the coaſt neere the ſhoꝛe: who returning to vs about one of the clock at after noone, declared that they had founde among other thinges viii. fadome of water at the harde bancke of the ſea. Wherevpon hauing diligently wayed vp our Anckers, and hoyſted vp our ſayles with wind at will, we ſayled and vewed the coaſt all along with vnſpeable pleaſure, of the odoꝛous ſmell and brawtte of the ſame. And becauſe there appeared vnto vs no ſigne of any Poꝛte, about the ſetting of the ſunne we caſt ancker againe: which done, we did behold to and fro the goodly oꝛder of the woods wherewith God hath decked euery way the ſayd land. Then perceiuing towarde the Noꝛth a leaping and a bꝛeaking of the water, as a ſtreame falling out of the lande into the Sea. Foꝛ the whiche wee ſet vp ſayles againe to double the ſame while it was yet day. And as wee had ſo done, and paſſed beyond it: there appeared vnto vs a fayꝛe entrie of a faire riuer which cauſed vs to caſt Ancker agayne there neuer the land: to the end the next day we might ſee what it was, and though that the winde blew foꝛ a time vehemently to the ſhoꝛeward: yet the hold and Anckerrage was ſo good, that one cable and one Ancker helde vs faſt, with out danger oꝛ ſliding.

The next day in the moꝛning, being the firſt of May, wee aſſayed to enter this Poꝛte, with two newe barges and a boate well trimmed, finding little water barges whiche might haue aſtonied and cauſed vs to returne backe to ſhipboꝛde, if God had not ſpeedily bꝛought vs in. Where finding 3 6. fadome water, entred into a goodly and great riuer, which

which as we went founde to encrease still in depth & large-
nesse,boyling and roaring through the multitude of all kind
of fish. This being entred wee perceiued a great number of
ÿ Indians inhabitants there,comming along the sandes &
Sea bankes,comming neare vnto vs, without any taking
of feare or doubt,shewing vnto vs the easiest landing place:
& thereupon we giuing them also on our parts thanks of assurance and friendlinesse. Forthwith one of appearance,out
of the best among them, brother vnto one of their kinges,or
gouernours,commaunded one of the Indians to enter into
the water : and to approch our boates to shew vs the coastes
landing place. We seeing this(without any more doubting
or difficultie)landed,and the messenger(after we had rewarded him with some looking glasse,and other pretie things of
small value)ran incontinently toward his Lord:Who forth
with sent mee his girdle, in token of assuraunce and friendship,which girdle was made of red leather, as well couered
and coloured as was possible:and as I began to go towards
him,hee set foorth and came and receiued me gently,and rei-
sed after his maner all his men,following with great silence
and modestie : yea more then our men did. And after we had
a while with gentle vsage congratulated with him : we fell
to the grounde a litle way from them,to call vpon the name
of God,and to beseech him to continue still his goodnesse towards vs,and bring to the knowledge of our sauiour Christ
this poore people. While wee were thus praying (they sitting vpon the grounde,which was strawed and dressed with
Bay bowes)behelde and hearkened vnto vs, very attentiue-
ly without either speking or mouing: and as I made a signe
vnto their king,lifting vp mine arme,and stretching foorth
one finger,only to make them looke vp to heauen warde:He
likewise lifting vp his arme towards heauen put foorth two
fingers:whereby it seemed that he made vs to vnderstande,
that they worshipped the Sunne and ÿ moone for Gods:as
afterwardes wee vnderstoode it so . In the meane time
their numbers increased, & thither came the kings brother,
that was first with vs,their mother, wiues, sisters and chil-

dren,and being thus assembled,they caused a great number
of Bay boughes to bee cut,and therewith a place to be dressed for vs,distant from theirs two fadom. For it is their maner to talke and bargaine sitting: and the chiefe of them to
bee apart,from the meaner sort,with a shewe of great obe-
dience to their kinges,superiours,and elders. They bee all
naked,and of a goodly stature,mightie, & as well shapen &
proportioned of body,as any people in ye world: very gentle,
curteous, and of a good nature.

The most part of them couer their raines and priuities
with faire Harts skinnes,painted most commonly with sundrie colours : and the fore part of their body and armes,bee
painted with pretie deuised workes, of Azure, red, and
blacke, so well and so properly as the best Painter of Europe coulde not amende it. The women haue their bodies painted with a certaine Herbe like vnto Mosse, whereof the Cedar trees,and all other trees bee alwayes couered.
The men for pleasure doe alwayes trimme them selues
therwith,after sundrie fashions: They bee of tauny colour,
hauke nosed,and of a pleasant countenance. The women be
well fauoured,and will not suffer one dishonestly to approch
too neare them. But wee were not in their houses for we
sawe none at that time.

After we had taried in this North side of the riuer the
Why the riuer
of May was so
called. most part of the day(which riuer wee haue called May, for
that wee discouered the same the firste day of the Moneth)
wee congratulated, made aliaunce, and entred into amitie with them,and presented the king and his brethren with
Gownes of ble we cloth garnished with yellowe Floure-de-
luces. And it seemed that they were sory for our departure:
so that the most part of them entred into the water vp to the
necke,to set our boates a flote.

Putting into vs sundry kinde of fishes,which with merueilous speede they ranne to take in their packs,made in the
water with great Reedes,so well and cunningly set togeather,after the fashion of a Laberinth,or Maze,with so many
turnes

turnes and crookes, as it is impossible to do it without much cunning and industrie.

But desiring to imploy the rest of the day on the other side of this riuer, to viewe and know those Indians that wee sawe there. We trauersed thither, and without any difficultie landed amongest them, who receiued vs very gently and with great humanitie: putting vs of their fruites, euen into our boates, Mulberies, Raspis, and such other fruites as they founde ready by the way.

Soone after this came thither the king with his brethren, and others with bowes and arrowes in their handes, vsing therewithall a goodly and a graue fashion, with their behauiour right souldierlike, and as warlike boldnes as may be. They were naked and painted as the other, their haire likewise long, and trussed vp (with a lace made of herbes) to the top of their heads: but they had neither their wiues nor children in their companie. After we had a good while louingly entertemed and presented them with like gifts of habersher wares, cutting hookes and hatchets, and clothed the king & his brethren with like robes, as we had giuen to them on the other side: we entred and viewed the countrie thereaboutes, which is the fairest, fruitfullest, & pleasantest of al the world, abounding in hony, venison, wilde foule, forests, woods of all sortes, Palme trees, Cypresse and Cedars, Bayes ye highest and greatest, with also the fayrest vines in all the world, with grapes according, which without natural art and without mans helpe or trimming will grow to toppes of Okes, and other trees that be of a wonderfull greatnesse & height. And the sight of the faire medowes is a pleasure not able to be expressed with tongue: full of Hernes, Curlues, Bitters, Mallards, Egrepths, woodcocks, & all other kinde of small birds: with Harts, Hindes, Buckes, wilde Swine, and all other kindes of wilde beastes, as we perceiued well both by their footing there, and also afterwardes in other places, by their crie and roaring in the night.

Also there be Conies & Hares: Silke wormes in merueilous number, a great deale fairer and better, then be our silk

wormes,

wormes. To bee ſhort, it is a thing vnſpeakeable to conſider the thinges that bee ſeene there, and ſhalbe founde more and more, in this incomperable lande, which neuer yet broken with plough prons, bringeth forth al things according to his firſt nature, wherewith the eternall God indued it. About their houſes they labour and till the grounde, ſowing their fieldes with a graine called Mahis, whereof they make their meale: and in their Gardens they plant beanes, gourdes, cucumbers, Citrons, peaſon, and many other fruits and rootes vnknowen vnto vs . Their ſpades and mattockes be made of Wood, ſo well and fitly as is poſſible: which they make with certaine ſtones, oyſter ſhelles & muſcles, wherewith alſo they make their bowes and ſmal launces: and cut & poliſh al! ſortes of wood, that they imploye about their buildings, and neceſſarie vſe: There groweth alſo many Walnut trees, Haſell trees, Cheritrees, very faire and great.

And generally wee haue ſeene, thereof the ſame ſimples and herbes that wee haue in Fraunce, and of the like goodneſſe, ſauour and taſte. The people be very good archers, and of great ſtrength: Their bowe ſtringes are made of Leather, and their arrowes of Reedes which they doe head with the teeth of fiſhes. As we now demaunded of them concerning ẙ land called Seuola, whereof ſome haue written not to bee farre from thence, and to bee ſituate within the lande, and toward the Sea called the South Sea. They ſhewed vs by ſignes that which we vnderſtood well enough, that they might goe thither with their Boates (by riuers) in twentie dayes. They that haue written of this kingdome and towne of Seuola, and other townes and kingdomes thereaboutes, ſay, that there is great aboundance of golde and ſiluer, precious ſtones, and other great riches: and that the people had their arrowes headed (in ſteede of yron) with ſharpe poi nted Turqueſſes. Thus the night approching, it was conuenient for vs to returne by day a ſhipboorde. Wee tooke leaue of them muche to their griefe, but more to ours without compariſon , for that wee had

Seuola within xx. daies trauailing by boate of the riuer of May.

had no meane to enter the riuers with our shippe. And albeit, it was not their custome eyther to eate oz dzinke from the Sunne rising till his going downe: yet the king openly woulde needes dzinke with vs, praying vs verie gently to giue him the cuppe whereout we had dzunke: and so making him to vnderstande that wee woulde see him againe the next day, we retired to our shippes, which lay aboue sixe leagues from the hauen to the sea.

The next day in the mozning we returned to land againe, accompanied with the Captaines, Gentlemen, and Souldiers, and other of our small trope: carying with vs a Pillour oz columne of harde stone, our kings armes graued therein, to plant and set the same in the enterie of the Pozte in some high place, where it might bee easely seene, and being come thither befoze the Indians were assembled, we espied on the south syde of the Riuer a place very fitte foz that purpose, vpon a litle hill, compassed with Cyprez, Bayes, Paulmes and other trees, with sweete smelling and pleasant shzubbes. In the middle whereof we planted the first bound oz limit of his Maiestie. This donz perceiuing our first Indians assembled, not without some misliking of those on the South parte, where we had set the limitte, who taried foz vs in the same place where they met with vs the day befoze, seeming vnto vs that there is some enimitie betweene them and the others. But when they percepued our long tarying on this syde, they ran to see what we had done in that place where we landed first, and had set our limitte: which they vewed a great while without touching it any way, oz abassing, oz euer speaking to vs therof at any time after. Howebeit we could skät depart but as it were wt griefe of minde frō this our first alliance, they rowing vnto vs all along the riuer from all parts and pzesenting vs with some of their harts skins, painted and vnpainted, meale, litle cakes, freshe water, rootes like vnto Rinbabe which they haue in great estimation, and make therof a potion of medicine: also they bzought litle bagges of redde colours and some small spices like vnto Aire, percey-

uing

tiug among them selues fayre thinges painted as it had bin with graine of scarlet, showing vnto vs by signes that they had in the lande golde and siluer and copper : whereof wee haue brought some. Also lead like vnto ours which we shewed. Also turquesses and great aboundance of pearles whiche as they declared vnto vs they tooke out of oysters, whereof there is taken euer along the riuer side, & among the reedes, and in the marshes : and so merueylous aboundance as is skant credible: and we haue perceiued that there be as many and as faire pearles found there as in any countrey of the worlde. For wee sawe a man of theirs as we entered into our boates, that had a pearle hanging at a coller of golde and siluer about his necke, as great as an Acorne at ý least. This man as he had taken fishe in one of their fishing packs thereby brought that same to our boates, and our men perceiuing the greatnesse therof, one of them putting his finger toward it, the man drewe backe, and woulde no more come neare the boate : not for any feare that he had that they woulde haue taken his Coller & Pearle from him for he would haue giuen it them, for a looking glasse or a knife:

But that hee doubted lest they woulde haue pulled him into the boate, & so by force haue caried him away. He was one of the goodliest men of all the company. But for that we had no leasure to tary any longer with them, the day being well passed, whiche greeued vs, for the commoditie and great riches, whiche as wee vnderstoode and sawe might bee gotten there, desiring also to employ the rest of the day with our seconde aliance the Indians on the southside, as we perceiued them the day before, which still taried looking for vs : Wee passed the riuer to their shore, where as wee founde them tarying for vs, quietly and in good order, with newe paintings vpon their face, and feathers vpon their heades: the King with his Bowe and Arrowes lying by him, sate on the grounde strawed with boughes betweene his two brethren, whiche were goodly men and well shapen and of a wonderfull show of actiuities, hauing vpon their heades, one haire trussed vp-

Gold, siluer, and copper in Florida.
Turquesses and aboundance of pearles.
Marshes.

Pearles as big as acornes.

vpright of heyght, of some kinde of wild beast gathered and
wrought together with great cunning, wethed and fasted
after the forme of a Diademe. One of them had hanging a-
bout his necke a rounde plate of redde copper well polished, with one other lesser of Siluer in the middest of it, & at
his eare a litle plate of Copper wherewith they vse to stripe
the sweat from their bodies. They shewed vs that there was
great store of this mettell within the countrey, about fiue or
sixe daies iourney from thence, both in the southside & northside of the same riuers, and that they went thither in their
Boates.   Which Boates they make but of one piece of a
tree, woorking it whole so cunningly and featly, that they
put in one of these boates fifteene or twentie persons, and go
their wayes very safely. They that rowe stande vpright hauing their ores short after the fashion of a Peele. Thus being
among them they presented vs with meale dressed & baked,
very good & wel tasted, and of good nourishmēt, also beanes,
and fish, as crabbes, lobstars, creuises, and many other kinde
of good fishes, shewing vs by signes ÿ their dwellings were
farre off, and if their prouision had been neere hande, they
woulde haue presented vs with manye other refresh-
inges.

  The night nowe approching, we were faine to returne
to our Shippe, very much to our griefe: for that wee durste
not hazarde to enter with our Shippe, by reason of a barre
of sande, that was at the enterie of the Porte, howe be it, at
a full Sea there is two fadome and a halfe of water at the
least, and it is but a leape ouer a surge to passe this Barre,
not passing the length of two cables, and then forthwith e-
uery where within sixe or seuen fadome water. So that it
maketh a very fayre hauen, and Shippes of a meane burden
from fourescore to a hundred tunnes may enter therein at all
floodes, yea of a farre greater burthen, if there were French
men dwelling there that might skoure the enterie as they
doe in Fraunce: for there is nothing lacking for the
lyfe of man. The situation is vnder the eleuation of xxx.
degrees, a good climate healthfull, and of a good

tem-

temperature, merueilous pleaſãt, ỹ people good, & of a good and amiable nature, which willingly will obay: yea be content to ſerue thoſe that ſhall with gentlenes and humanitie goe about to allure them, as it is needful for thoſe that be ſent thither hereafter ſo to doe, and as I haue charged thoſe that be left there to do, to the ende they may aſke and learne of thẽ where they take their gold, copper, and turqueſſes, and other thinges yet vnknowen vnto vs; by reaſon of the time we ſoiourned there. For if any rude or rigorous meanes ſhould be vſed towards this people, they woulde flie hither and thither through the Woods and Foreſts, and abandon their habitations and countreys.

Gentlenes muſt be vſed towards them.

The next day being the thirde day of May, deſiring alwaies to finde out harbours to reſt in, we ſet vp ſaile againe: And after we had raunged the coaſt as neere the ſhore as we could, there appeared vnto vs about ſeuen leagues of on this ſide of ỹ riuer of May a great opening or Bay of ſome riuer, whither with one of our boates we rowed, & there found one entrie almoſt like ỹ of the riuer of May, and within the ſame as great a depth, and as large a diuiding it ſelfe into many great ſtreames, great and broade ſtretchinges towardes the high lande, with many other leſſe, that diuide the countrey into faire and great landes and great number of ſmall and fayre Medowes. Being entred vnto them about three leagues, wee found in a place very commodious, ſtrong, and pleaſant of ſituation, certayne Indians, who receiued vs very gently: Howe be it, we being ſomewhat neare their houſes, it ſeemed it was ſomewhat againſt their good willes that we went thither, for at their cries and noyſes they made their wiues and children and hoſhoulde ſtuffe to be caried into the Woods: Howe be it they ſuffered vs to goe into their houſes, but they themſelues woulde not accompany vs thither. Their houſes bee made of Wood fitly and cloſe, ſet vpright and couered with Reedes: the moſt part of them after the faſhion of a pauilion. But there was one houſe amongeſt the reſt verie long and broade, with ſettles rounde about made

of

of Reedes trimly couched together, which serue them both
for beddes and seates, they be of height two foote from the
grounde, set vpon great rounde pillers painted with red, yelowe, and blewe, well and trimlie polished: some sorte of this
people perceiuing that we had in no maner wise hurted their
dwellings nor gardens whiche they dressed very diligently,
they returned all vnto vs before our inbarking, seeming very
well contented by their giuing vnto vs water, fruites, and
Hart skinnes. It is a place wonderfull fertill, and of strong
situatiõ, the ground fat, so that it is likely that it would bring
forth Wheate and all other corne twise a yeere, and the commodities for liuelihood, and the hope of more riches, bee like
vnto those we found and considered vpon the riuer of May,
without comming into the sea : this arme doth diuide, and
maketh many other Iles of May, as also many other great
Ilandes : by the which wee trauell from one Ilande to another, betweene lande and land. And it seemeth that men may
sayle without danger through al the countrey, and neuer enter into the great sea, which were a wonderfull aduantage.

Great fertillitie.

Note.

This is the lande of Checere whereof some haue written,
& which many haue gone about to find out, for ye great riches
they perceiued by some Indians to be founde there. It is set
vnder so good a climate, that none of our men (though wee
were there in the hotest time of the yeere, the sunne entring
into Cancer) were troubled with any sieknesses. The people
there liue long and in great health and strength, so that the a-
ged men goe without staues, and are able to goe and runne
like the youngest of them, who onely are knowen to be olde
by the wrinckles in their face, and decay of sight. Wee departed from them verie friendly, & with their contentation.
But the night ouertaking vs, we were constrayned to lye in
our ships all that night, till it was day, floting vpon this riuer which we haue called Sene, because that the entery of
it is as broade as from hauer degrace vnto Honesleue. At
the breake of the day wee espied out of the South syde one
of the fayrest, pleasauntest, and greatest medowe grounde

The riuer of
Sene.

G   that

that might bee ſeene, into the which wee went, finding at the very entrie a long, faire, and great Lake, and an innumera‐ ble number of footeſteps of great Hartes and Hindes of a wonderfull greatneſſe, the ſteppes beeing all freſh and new, and it ſeemeth that the people doe nouriſhe them like tame Cattell in great heards: for we ſaw the ſteppes of an Indian that folowed them.

Heardes of tame Hartes.

The Chanell and depth of this riuer of Seyne, is one ye ſide of the medowe that is in the Iſle of May. Being retur‐ ned to our ſhips, we ſayled to knowe more and more of this coaſt, goying as neeve the ſhore as we coulde. And as wee had ſayled about ſixe or ſeuen leagues, there appeared vnto vs another Bay, where we caſt anker, and tarrying ſo all the night, in the morning wee went thither, and finding (by our ſounding) at the entrie many bankes and beatings, we durſt not enter there with our great ſhip, hauing named the riuer Somme, which is 8.9.10.11.fadome depth, diuiding it ſelfe into many great Ilands, and ſmall goodly medow grounds and paſtures, and euery where ſuch abundance of fiſh as is incredible, and on the Weaſt Northweſt ſide, there is a great riuer that commeth fro the countrie of a great length ouer : and another on the Northeaſt ſide, which returne into the Sea. So that (my Lord) it is a countrie full of hauens, ri‐ uers, and Ilands, of ſuch fruitfulnes as cannot with tongue be expreſſed : and where in ſhort time great and precious co‐ modities might bee found. And beſides this wee diſcouered and found alſo vii.riuers more, as great and as good, cutting and diuiding the land into faire and great Ilands. The In‐ dians inhabitants there be like in manners, & the countrie in fertillitie apt and commodious throughout to beare & bring foorth plentifully all that men would plant or ſowe vpon it. There bee euery where the higheſt and greateſt Firtrees ye can be ſeene, very well ſmelling, and whereout might bee gathered (with cutting the only bark) as much Roſen, Tur‐ pentine, & Frankeſence, as men would deſire. And to be ſhort there lacketh nothing. Wherefore being not able to enter & lie with our great veſſels there, we could make no long abi‐ ding.

Good hauens and riuers.

7.Great & good riuers.

ding, nor enter so farre into the riuers and countries as wee would faine haue done: for it is well knowne how many inconueniences haue happened vnto men, not only in attempting of newe discoueries, but also in all places by leauing their great vessels in the Sea, farre from the land, vnfurnished of the heads and best men. As for ye other riuers we haue giuen them names as followeth: and vnto the Ilandes ioyning vnto them, the same name that the next riuer vnto it hath, as you shall see by the portratures or Cardes ye I haue made thereof. As to the fourth name of Loire, to ye fift Charnet, to ye sixt Caro to the 7. riuer Belle, to ye 8. riuer Graude, to the 9. port Royall, and to the tenth Belle Uirrir.

Maps and Sea Cardes.

Upon Whitsunday the xxvii. day of May, after wee had perceiued and considered that there was no remedie, but to assay to find the meanes to harber our ships, as wel to amend and trimme them, as to get vs fresh water, wood, and other necessaries, whereof wee hauing opinion that there was no fayrer or fitter place for the purpose, then port Royall. And when wee had sounded the entrie and the Chanell (thanked be God) wee entered safely therein with our shippes, against the opinion of many, finding the same one of the fayrest and greatest Hauens of the worlde.

Port royall a most excellent hauen.

Howe be it, it must be remembred least men approching neare it within seuen leagues of the lande, bee abashed and afraide on the Eastside, drawing towarde the Southeast, the grounde to be flatte, for neuerthelesse at a full sea, there is euery where foure fadome water, keeping the right Chanel.

Note.

In this part there are many riuers of meane bignesse and large, where without daunger the greatest shippes of the worlde might bee harboured, which wee founde, no Indian inhabiting there aboutes. The Porte and Riuers side is neerer then tenne or twelue leages vpwardes into the countreys, although it bee one of the goodliest, best, and fruitefullest countreys that euer was seene, and where nothing lacketh, and also whereas good and likely commodities bee founde as in other places thereby.

For wee founde there a great number of Pepertrees,

Pepper trees

the

the Pepper yet greene, and not ready to bee gathered: Also the beſt water of the world, and ſo many ſortes of fiſhes that yee may take them without net or angle ſo many as ye will. Also an innumerable ſort of wilde foule of all ſortes, and in little Ilandes at the entrie of this hauen, on the Eaſt North eaſt ſide, there is ſo great number of Egrepes that the buſhes bee all white and couered with them, ſo that one may take of the young ones with his hande as many as hee will carry away. There bee also a number of other foules, as Vernes, Bitters, Curlues. And to bee ſhort, there is ſo many ſmall byrdes that it is a ſtrange thing to bee ſeene. Wee founde the Indians there more doubtfull and fearefull then the others before: Yet after we had been in their houſes, and congregated with them, and ſhewed curteſie to thoſe that we founde to haue abandoned there through boats meale, victuall, and ſmall houſholde ſtuffe, and both in not taking away or touching any part thereof, and in leauing in that place
A ſpeciall note. where they dreſſed their meate, Kniues, Looking glaſſes, little Beades of glaſſe, which they loue and eſteeme aboue golde and pearles, for to hang them at their eares and neck, and to giue them to their wiues and children : they were ſomewhat emboldened.

For ſome of them came to our boates, of the which wee carried two goodly and ſtrong aboorde our ſhippes, clothing and vſing them as gently as it was poſſible. But they ceaſed not day nor nyght to lament, and at length they eſcaped away. Wherefore albeit, I was willing (according to your commaundement and memoriall) to bring away ſome of
A commande ment. them with vs, on the Princes behalfe and yours, I forbare to doe ſo for many conſiderations and reaſons that they told mee, and for that we were in doubt that (leauing ſome of our men there to inhabite) all the Countrie, men, women, and children, woulde not haue ceaſed to purſue them for to haue theirs againe : ſeeing they bee not able to conſider and way to what entent wee ſhoulde haue carried them away : & this may bee better doone to their contentation, when they haue better acquaintance of vs, and know that there is no ſuche
crueltie

crueltie in vs, as in other people and nations, of whom they haue beene beguiled vnder colour of good faith: whiche doing in the ende turned to the doers no good. This is the riuer of Iordain in mine opinion, whereof so much hath beene spoke, which is very faire & the coūtrie good, both for ȳ easie habitation, and also for many other things, which should bee long to write. The riuer of Iordan.

The twentie of May wee planted another columne or pillor grauen with the kinges armes on the South side, in a high place, of the entrie of a great riuer, which wee called Libourne: where there is a lake of fresh water very good, and on the same side a little lower towards the entrie of the Hauen is one of the fayrest fountaines that a man may drink of, which falleth by violence down to the riuer from an high place out of a red and sandy ground, and yet for all that fruitefull and of good ayre, where it shoulde seeme that the Indians haue had some faire habitation.

There we sawe the fayrest & the greatest vines with grapes according, and young trees, and smal woods, very wel smelling, that euer were seen: wherby it appeareth to be the pleasantest & most commodious dwelling of al ȳ world. Wherefore (my Lorde) trusting you will not thinke it amisse (considering the commodities that may be brought thence) if we leaue a number of men there, which may fortifie and prouide them selues of things necessary: for in all new discoueries it is the chiefest thing that may be done, at the beginning to fortifie and people the countrey. I had not so soone set forth this to our companie, but many of them affraid to tary there, yet with such a good will and ioly corage, that such a number did thus offer themselues, as we had much to do to stay their importunitie. Exceeding faire and great vines Fortification most necessarie in all newe discoueries.

And namely of our shipmaisters and principall pilotes, and such as we could not spare. How bee it, wee lefte there but to the number of thirtie in all, Gentlemen, souldiers, and marriners, and that at their own suit and prayer, and of their owne free willes, and by the aduice and deliberation of the Gentlemen sent on the behalfe of the Prince and yours. 30. lefte behind at their owne suits

And

And haue left vnto the forehead and rulers (following therein your good will) Captaine Albert de la Pierria, a ſouldier of long experience, and the firſt that from the beginning did offer to tarry. And further by theyr aduice, choyſe

They fortified in an Iland.

and will, inſkaled and fortified them in an Iland on the north ſide, a place of ſtrong ſituation and commomodious, vpon a riuer which wee named Chenonceau, and the habitation and Fortreſſe Charlefote.

After we had inſtructed and duly admoniſhed them of that they ſhoulde doe (as well for their maner of proceeding, as for the good and louing behauiour of them) the xi. day of the moneth of June laſt paſt, we departed from port Royal: minding yet to range and view the coaſt vntill the xl. degrees of

Fortie degrees of eleuation.

the eleuation: But for as much as there came vpon vs troubleſome and cloudie weather, very incommodious for our purpoſe, and conſidering alſo amongſt many other thinges, that we had ſpent our cables and furniture thereof, which is the moſt principall thing that longeth to them that go to diſcouer countreys, where continually both night and day they muſt lie at ancker: alſo our victualls beeing periſhed and ſpilte, our lacke of Boateſwaines to ſet forth our rowe barges, and leaue our veſſels furniſhed. The declaration made vnto vs of our Pilots and ſome others that had before been at ſome of thoſe places, where we purpoſed to ſayle, and haue been already found by ſome of the kings ſubiects, the daunger alſo and inconueniences that might thereof happen vnto

Miſtes & fogs when they come.

vs: & by reaſon of the great myſtes and fogges wherof the ſeaſo was already come, we perceiued very well wheras we were, ŷ we could do no good, & that it was to late, & ŷ good & fit ſeaſon for to vndertake this thing already paſt. Al theſe thinges thus well conſidered and wayed, and alſo for that we thought it meet and neceſſarie that your honour ſhould with diligence be aduertiſed (through the help of God) to returne homewards to make relatiō vnto you of the effect of our nauigation. Praying God that it may pleaſe him to keepe you in long health, and proſperitie.

FINIS.

Notes in writing besides more

ptiuie by mouth that were giuen by a Gentleman,
Anno, 1580. *to* M. *Arthure Pette and to* M. *Charles Iack-*
man, sent by the marchants of the Muscouie companie for the
discouerie of the northeast strayte, not altogether vnfit
for some other enterprises of discouerie, hereaf-
ter to bee taken in hande.

What respect of Ilandes is to be had, and why.

Hereas the Portingales haue in their
course to their Indies in the Southeast,
certaine portes and fortificatiōs to thrust
into by the way, to diuers great purposes: So you are to see what Ilands, and
what portes you had neede to haue by the
way in your course to the Northeast. For which cause I
wish you to enter into consideration of the matter, & to note
all the Ilands, & to set them downe in plat, to two endes, that
is to say, That wee may deuise to take the benefite by them.
And also foresee how by thē the Sauages or ciuill Princes,
may in any sort annoy vs in our purposed trade that way.

And for that the people to the which wee purpose in this
voyage to goe, be no Chrstians, it were good that the masse
of our commodities were alwayes in our owne disposition,
and not at the will of others. Therefore it were good that
we did seeke out some small Iland in the Scithian Sea,
where we might plant, fortifie, & Staple safely, frō whēce
(as time should serue) wee might feede those heathen
nations with our commodities without cloying them, or
without venturing our hole masse in the bowels of their
countrey.

And to whiche Ilande if neede were (and if we shoulde
thinke so good) we might allure the Northeast nauie, the nauie of Cambalu to resort with their commodities to vs there
planted, and stapling there.

And

And if such an Iland might be found so standing as might shorten our course, and so standing, as that the Nauie of Cābalu, or other those parties might coueniently saile vnto without their dislike in respect of distāce: thē would it fal out wel. For so, besides lesse dāger, and more safetie, our ships might there vnlade and lade againe, and returne the selfe same som̄mer to the ports of England or of Norway.

And if such an Iland may be found for the stabling of our commodities, to the which they of Cambalu would not saile, yet we might, hauing shippes there, imploy them in passing betweene Cambalu and that stapling place.

Respect of hauens and harbarowes.

ANd if no such Ilandes may be found in the Scithiā sea toward the firme of Asia, then are you to search out the ports that be about Noua Sembla all along the tract of that land, to the end you may winter there the first yeere, if you be let by contrarie winds, & to the ende that if wee may in short time come vnto Cābalu, & vnlade and set saile againe for returne without venteriug, there at Cābalu, that you may on your way come as farre in returne as a port about Noua Sēbla: That the Sommer following, you may the sooner be in England for the more speedy vent of your East cōmodities, and for the speedier discharge of your Mariners: if you can not goe forward and backe in one selfe same sommer.

And touching the tract of the land of Noua sembla, toward the East out of the circle Artick in the more temperate zone, you are to haue regard, for if you finde the soyle planted with people, it is like þ in time an ample vēt of our warm wollē clothes may be founde. And if there be no people at al there to be found, then you shall specially note what plentie of whales, & of other fish is to be found there, to the end wee may turne our newfoūd land fishing or Island fishing, or our whalefishing, þ way for the ayde & cōfort of our new trades to the Northeast, to the coasts of Asia.

Respect of fishe and certayne other thinges.

And if the ayre may be found vpon that tract temperate, & the soyle peelding wood, water, land and grasse, and the seas fish, then we may plant on that mayne the offals of our people, as the Portingals doe in Brasil, & so they may in our fishing in our passage, & diuers wayes peelde commoditie to England by harbouring and vitelling of vs.

And it may bee, that the inland there may peelde mastes, pitch, tarre, hempe, and all thinges for the Nauie, as plentifully as Eastland doth.

The Ilandes to be noted with their commodities and wantes.

To note the Ilands, whether they be hie lande or lowe land, moūtanie, or flat, sandy, grauelly, clay, chalchy, or of what soyle, wooddy or not wooddy, with springs & riuers or not, and what wyld beasts they haue in the same.

And whether there seeme to be in the same apt matter to build withall, as stone free or rough, and stone to make lime withall, and wood or coale to burne the same withall.

To note the goodnes or the badnes of the hauens, & harborowes in the Ilandes.

If a straite be founde what is to bee done and what greate importance it may bee of.

And if there be a strayte in the passage into the Scithian Seas, the same is specially and with great regard to bee noted, especially if the same straite be narrow and to be kept, I say it is to be noted as a thing that doeth much importe, for what Prince soeuer shall be Lorde of the same, and shall possesse the same, as the king of Denmarke doth possesse the straite of Denmarke, he onely shall haue the trade out of these regions into the Northeast partes of the world for himselfe, and for his priuate profit, or for his subiectes only, or to enioy wonderfull benefite of the toll of the same, like as the king of Dēmarke doth enioy of his straites, by suffering the Merchantes of other Princes to passe that way, If any such straite be found, the eleuation, the hie or lowe lande, the ha-

uens

uens neere, the length of the ſtraites, & all other ſuch circũ-
ſtaunces are to be ſet downe for many purpoſes : And all the
Mariners in ẙ voyage are to be ſworne to keepe cloſe al ſuch
thinges, that other Princes preuent vs not of the ſame, after
our returne vpon the diſcloſing of the mariners, if any ſuch
thing ſhould happe.

Which way the Sauage may be made able to purchaſe our cloth and other their wantes.

IF you finde any Iland or mayne lande populous, and that
the ſame people hath neede of cloth : Then are you to deuiſe what commodities they haue to purchaſe the ſame
withall.

If they be poore, then are you to conſider of the ſoyle, and
how by any poſſibilitie the ſame may be made to enrich thẽ,
that hereafter they may haue ſomthing to purchaſe the cloth
withall.

If you enter into any mayne by portable riuer, and ſhall
finde any great woodds, you are to note what kynd of timber
they be of : That we may know whether they are for pitche,
tarre, maſtes, deleborde, clapborde, or for buylding of ſhips or
houſes, for ſo if the people haue no vſe of them they maye be
brought perhaps to vſe.

Not to venture the loſſe of any one man.

YOu muſt haue great care to preſerue your people, ſince
your number is ſo ſmall, and not to venture any one
man in any wiſe.

To bring home beſides marchandize certaine trifles.

BRing home with you (if you may) from Cambalu, or o-
ther ciuill place, one or other young man, although you
leaue one for him.

Alſo the fruites of the countries, if they will not of themſelues
dure, drie them, and ſo preſerue them.

And bring with you the Curnelles of peres, & apples, and
the ſtones of ſuch ſtone fruites as you ſhall finde there.

Also the seedes of all strange herbes and flowres, for such seedes of fruites and hearbes comming from another part of the world and so farre off, wil delite the fancie of many, for the strangenes and for that the same may growe and continue the delite long time.

If you arriue at Cambalu or Quinsay, to bring thence the Mappe of that Countrey, for so shall you haue the perfecte description which is to great purpose.

To bring thence some old printed booke, to see whether they haue had print there, before it was deuised in Europe as some write.

To note their force by sea and by lande.

If you arriue in Cambalu or Quinsay, to take a speciall viewe of their Nauie, and to note the force, greatnesse, maner of building of them, the sayles, the tackels, the anckers, the furniture of them, with ordinaunce, armour, and munition.

Also, to note the force of the walles and bulwarkes of their cities, their ordinaunce, and whether they haue any caliuers, and what powder and shot.

To note what armour they haue.

What swordes.

What pikes, halbertes and billes.

What horses of force, and what light horses they haue.

And so throughout, to note the force of the countrey, both by sea and by lande.

Things to be marked to make coniectures by.

To take speciall note of their buildings, and of the ornaments of their houses within.

Take a speciall note of their apparell and furniture, & of the substance that the same is made of, of which a marchant may make a gesse, as well of their commodities as also of their wantes.

To note their shoppes and warehouses and with what

commo=

commodities they abounde, the price alfo.

To fee their fhambles, and to viewe all fuch thinges as are brought into the markets, for fo you fhall fone fee the commodities, and the maner of the people of the inlande, and fo giue a geffe of many things.

To note their fieldes of grayne, and their trees of fruite, and howe they abounde or not abounde in one and other, and what plentie or fcarcetie of fifhe they haue.

Thinges to be carried with you, whereof more or leffe is to be caried for a fhewe of our commodities to bee made.

KErfies of all orient coulours, fpecially of ftamel, brode-cloth of orient colours alfo.

Frifadoes, motleys, briftowe frices, fpanifh blankettes, bayes of all collours, fpecially with ftanell, woffeds, carels, fayes, wedmoles, flanelles, rafhe, &c.

Feltes of diuers colours.

Taffeta hats.

Deepe cappes for mariners coloured in ftamell, whereof if ample vent may be found, it woulde turne to an infinite commoditie of the common poore people by knitting.

Quilted Cappes of leuant Taffeta of diuers colours, for the night.

Knit ftockes of filke of orient colours.

Knit ftockes of Ierfey yerne, of orient colours, whereof if ample vent might followe the poore multitude fhoulde be fet in worke.

Stocks of kerfey of diuers colours for men and for women.

Garters of Silke of feuerall kindes, and of colours diuers.

Girdels of Buffe, and all other leather, with gilt and vn-gilt Buckles, fpecially waft girdels, waft girdles of veluet.

Gloues of all fortes, knit and of leather.

Gloues perfumed.

Poyntes of all fortes of filke, thzeed, and lether, of all manner of colours.

Shooes of fpanifhe leather, of diuers colours, of diuers
lengthes, cut and vncut.

Shooes of other leather.

Ueluet shooes, and pantoples.

Thefe shooes and pantoples to be fent this time, rather for a showe then for any other caufe.

Purfes knit, and of leather.

Night cappes knit and other.

A Garnishe of Pewter, for a showe of a vent of that englishe commoditie, Bottelles, flagons, fpoones, &c. of that
metall.

Glaffes of englishe making.

Uenice glaffes.

Looking glaffes for women, great and fayre.

Small dials a few for proofe, although there they wil not
hold the order they do heere.

Spectacles of the common fort.

Others of Criftall trymmed with filuer and otherwife.

Owre glaffes.

Commes of Juorie.

Commes of Boxe.

Commes of Horne.

Linen of diuers forts.

Handkerchewes with filke of feuerall colours wrought.

Glafen eyes to ride with againft duft.

Kniues in sheathes, both fingle and double, of good edge.

Needles great and small of euery kinde.

Buttons greater and fmaller, with mouldes of leather
and not of wood, and fuch as be durable of double filke, and
that of fundrie colours.

Boxes with weightes of golde, and of euery kinde of the
coyne of golde, good and badde, to shewe that the people
here, vfe weight and measure whiche is a certayne showe
of wifedome, and of a certayne gouernment fetled here.

All the seuerall siluer Coynes of our Englishe moneys, to bee caried with you to bee showed to the gouernours at Cambalu, which is a thing that shal in silence speake to wise men more then you imagine.

Lockes and keyes, hinges, boltes, haspes, &c. great and small of excellent workemanshippe, whereof if vent may bee hereafter, wee shall set our subiectes in worke, whiche you must haue in great regarde. For in finding ample vente of any thing that is to be wrought in this realme, is more worth to our people besides the gaine of the marchant, then Christ-church, Bridewel, the Sauoy, and all the Hospitals of Eng-lande.

For banketing on Shipborde, persons of credite.

First the sweetest perfumes to set vnder hatches to make the place sweete against their comming aborde, if you ar-riue at Cambalu, Quinsey, or in such great cities and not a-mong sauages.

Marmelade.

Sucket.

Figges barelled.

Reysings of the sunne.

Comfets of diuers kindes made of purpose, that shall not dissolue by him that is most excellent.

Prunes damaske.

Dried peres.

Walnuttes.

Almondes.

Smalnuttes.

Oliues to make them taste their wine.

The Apple Iohn that dureth two yeeres to make showe of our fruites.

Hullocke.

Sacke.

Vials of good sweet waters, & casting bottels of glasses to besprinckel the gests withall, after their comming aborde.

Suger, to vse with their wine, if they will,   The

The sweete oyle of Sancie and excellent Frenche vineger, and a fine kinde of Bisket, stiped in the same doe make a banketting dishe, and a little Suger cast in it cooleth and comforteth, and refresheth the spirites of man.

Synomome water ⎫ is to be had with you to make a shew
Imperiall water ⎬ of by taste, and also to comfort your
　　　　　　　 ⎭ sicke in the voyage.

With these and such like, you may banket where you arriue the greater and best persons.

Or with the gift of these Marmelades in small boxes, or small violles of sweete waters you may gratifie by way of gift, or you may make a merchandise of them.

The mappe of England and of London.

Take with you the mappe of Englande set out in faire colours, one of the biggest sort I meane, to make shewe of your Countrie from whence you come.

And also the large mappe of London, to make shewe of your Citie. And let the riuer bee drawne full of shippes of all sortes, to make the more shewe of your greate trade and trafficke in trade of merchandise.

Ortelius booke of mappes

If you take Ortelius booke of mappes with you, to marke all these regions, it were not amisse, and if neede were to present the same to the great Cam, for it would bee to a Prince of merueilous account.

The booke of the attyre of all nations.

Such a booke carried with you and bestowed in gift, woulde be much esteemed, as I persuade my selfe.

Bookes.

If any man will lende you the newe Herball, and suche bookes as make shewe of Herbes, Plantes, Trees, Fishes, Foules and Beastes of these regions, it may much delight

the

the great Cam, and the nobilitie, and also their merchants to haue the viewe of them: for all things in these parties so much differing from the thinges of those regions, since they may not be here to see thē, by meane of the distance, yet to see those things in a shadowe, by this meane will delight them.

The booke of Rates.

TAke with you the booke of Rates, to the ende you may pricke all those commodities there specified that you shall chaunce to find in Cambalu, in Quinsey, or in any part of the East, where you shall chaunce to bee.

Parchment.

Rowles of Parchment, for that we may vent much without hurt to the Realme, and it lyes in small roome.

Glewe.

To carrye Glewe, for that wee haue plentie, and want vent.

Red Oker for Painters.

To seeke vent because wee haue great mines of it, and haue no vent.

Sope of both kindes.

To trie what vent it may haue, for that we make of both kindes, and may perhaps make more.

Saffron.

To trie what vent you may haue of Saffron, because this Realme yeeldes the best of the worlde, and for the tillage and other labours, may set the poore greatly in work to their reliefe.

Aquauitæ.

By newe deuise wonderfull quantities may bee made heere, and therefore to seeke the vent.

Blacke Conie skinnes.

To trie the vent at Cambalue, for that it lyes towardes

the

the North, and for that wee abounde with the commoditie, and may spare it.

Threade of all colours.

The vent thereof may set our people in worke.

Copper Spurres, and haukes belles.

To see the vent, for it may set our people in worke.

A note and a caueat for the merchant.

That before you offer your commodities to sale that you indeuour to learne what commodities the Countrie there hath. For if you bring thither veluet, taffeta, spice, or any such commoditie that you your selfe desire to lade your selfe home with, you must not sell yours deare, least hereafter you purchase theirs not so cheape as you woulde.

Seedes for sale.

Carrie with you for that purpose, all sortes of Garden seedes, as well of sweete strawing herbes and of flowers, as also of pot herbes, and all sorts for rootes, &c.

Leadde of the first melting.

Leadde of the second melting of the slagges.

To make triall of the vent of Leadde of all kindes.

English yron, and wyer of yron and copper.

To trye the sale of the same.

Brymstone.

To trie the vent of the same, because wee abounde of it made in the Realme.

Anthimoney a minerall.

To see whether they haue any ample use there for it, for that wee may lade whole nauies of it, and haue no vse of it vnlesse it bee for some small portion in founding of belles, or a lithel that the Alcumistes vse, of this you may haue two sortes at the Appoticaries,

Timber

Tinder boxes with Steele, flint, and matches, and tinder, the matches to bee made of Gineper, to auoide the offence of brimstone.

To trie and to make the better sale of Brimstone by shewing the vse.

Candles of waxe to light.

A painted Bellowes.

For that perhaps they haue not the vse of them.

A pot of cast yron.

To trie the sale, for that it is a naturall comoditie of this Realme.

All maner of edge tooles.

To bee sold there or to the lesse ciuill people by the way where you shall twich.

What I woulde haue you there to remember.

To note specially what excellent dying they vse in these regions, and therefore to note their garments, & ornaments of houses: and to see their die houses and the materialles, and simples that they vse about the same: and to bring Musters and shewes of the colours and of the materials, for that it may serue this clothing realme to great purpose.

To take with you for your owne vse.

All maner of Engyns to take fishe and foule.

To take with you those thinges that bee in perfection of goodnesse.

For as the goodnesse nowe at the first may make your commodities in credit in time to come : So false and sophisticate commodities shall drawe you and all your commodities into contempt and ill opinion.

❧ Notes framed by a Gentleman heretofore to bee giuen to one that pre-pared for a difcouerie, and went not: And not vnfitt to be committed to print, confidering the fame may ftirre vp confiderations of thefe and of fuch other thinges, not vnmeete in fuch new voyages as may be attempted hereafter.

That the firft Seate be chofen on ẙ feafide fo as (if it may be) you may haue your owne Na-uie within Bay, riuer oʒ lake, within your feat fafe from the enemie. And fo as the enemie fhalbe foʒced to lie in opē rode abʒoade without, to be difper-fed with all windes and tem-pefts that fhall arife. Thus feated you fhall bee leaft fubiecte to annoy of the enemie, fo may you by your Nauie within, paffe out to all partes of the woʒlde, and fo may the fhippes of Englande haue acceffe to you to fupply all wantes, fo may your commodities be cari-ed away alfo. This feate is to bee chofen in temperate Cli-mat, in fweete ayʒe, where you may poffeffe alwayes fweete water, wood, feacoles, oʒ turfe, with fifh, flefh, grayne, fruits, herbes and rootes, oʒ fo many of thofe, as may fuffice very necefsitie foʒ the life of fuch as fhall plant there. And foʒ the poffeffing of mines of golde, of filuer, copper, quickfiluer, oʒ of any fuche pꝛecious thing, the wantes of diuers of thofe needfull thinges may be fupplied from fome other place by fea, &c.

Stone to make Lyme of. Slate ftone to tile withall oʒ fuche clay as maketh tyle, Stone to wall withal if ⌐ are to be looked foʒ as thinges without which no Citie may bee made

K   noʒ

Brycke may not bee made, | nor people in ciuill sorte
   Timber for building ease= | be kept together.
ly to be conueied to the place,
   Reede to couer houses or
such like, if tile or slate be not.

The people there to plant and to continue are eyther to
liue without trafficke, or by trafficke and by trade of mar=
chandize. If they shall liue without sea trafficke, at the first
they become naked by want of linen and wollen, and very
miserable by infinite wantes that will otherwise ensue, and
so will they be forced of them selues to depart, or els easely
they will bee consumed by the Sp. by the Fr. or by the na=
turall inhabithantes of the countrey, and so the interprice
becomes reprochfull to our nation, and a lett to many o=
ther good purposes that may be taken in hande.

And by trade of marchandize they can not liue, excepte
the sea or the lande there may yeelde commoditie for com=
moditie. And therefore you ought to haue most speciall re=
garde of that point, and so to plant, that the naturall com=
modities of the place and seate, may drawe to you accesse of
Nauigation for the same, or that by your owne Nauigation
you may carie the same out, and fetche home the supplye
of the wantes of the seate.

Such nauigation so to bee employed, shall besides the
supply of wantes, bee able to encounter with forreyne force.

And for that in the ample vente of suche thinges as are
brought to you out of engl. by sea, standeth a matter of great
consequence, it behoueth that all humanitie and curtesie and
much forbearing of reuenge to the inland people be vsed, so
shall you haue firme amitie with your neyghbours, so shall
you haue their inland commodities to maintayne trafficke,
& so shall you waxe rich and strong in force. Diuers & seue=
rall commodities of the inland are not in great plentie to be
brought to your handes, without the ayde of some portable
or Nauigable ryuer, or ample lacke, and therefore to haue
the

the helpe of suche a one is most requisite : And so is it of effecte for the dispersing of your owne commodities in exchange into the inlandes.

Nothing is more to be indeuoured with the Inland people then familiaritie. For so may you best discouer al the naturall commodities of their countrey , and also all their wantes, all their strengthes, all their weakenesse, and with whome they are in warre, and with whome considerate in peace and amitie, &c. whiche knowen, you may woorke many great effectes of greatest consequence.

And in your planting the consideration of the climate and of the soyle bee matters that are to bee respected . For if it be so that you may let in the salt sea water, not mixed with the fresh into flattes , where the sunne is of the heate that it is at Rochell, in the Bay of portingall, or in Spaine , then may you procure a man of skill, and so you haue wonne one noble commoditie for the fishing , and for trade of marchandize by making of Salt.

Or if the soyle and clymate bee such as may yeelde you the Grape as good as that at Burdeus, as that in Portingale, or as that about Siui in Spaine, or that in the Ilands of the Canaries, then there resteth but a woorkeman to put in execution to make wines, and to dresse Resings of the sunne and other, &c.

Or if you finde a soyle of the temperature of the South part of Spaine or Barbarie, in whiche you finde the Olif tree to growe: Then you may bee assured of a noble marchandize for this realme, considering that our great trade of clothing doth require oyle, and weying howe deere of late it is become by the vent they haue of that commoditie in the West Indies, and if you finde the wilde olif there it may be graffed.

Or if you can finde the berrie of Cochenile with whiche wee colour Stammelles, or any Roote, Berrie, Fruite, wood or earth fitte for dying, you winne a notable thing fitt

for

for our ſtate of clothing. This Cochenile is naturall in the weſt Indies on that firme.

Or if you haue hides of beaſtes fit for ſole Lether, &c. It wilbe a marchandize right good, and the ſauages there yet can not tanne Lether after our kinde, yet excellently after their owne maner.

Or if the ſoyle ſhall yeeld Figges, Almondes, Sugar Canes, Quinces, Orenges, Lemons, Potatos, &c. there may ariſe ſome trade and trafficke, by figges, almonds, ſugar, marmelade, Sucket &c.

Or if great woods bee founde, if they be of Cypres, cheſts may bee made, if they bee of ſome kinde of trees, pitche and tarre may be made, if they bee of ſome other then they may yeelde Roſin, Turpentine, &c. and al for trade and trafficke, and Caſkes for wine and oyle may be made: likewiſe ſhips and houſes, &c.

And becauſe trafficke is a thing ſo materiall, I wiſh that great obſeruation be taken what euery ſoyle yeeldeth naturally, in what commoditie ſoeuer, and what it may be made to yeeld by indeuour, and to ſend vs notice home, that thereuppon wee may deuiſe what meanes may be thought of to rayſe trades.

Nowe admit that we might not be ſuffered by the ſauages to enioy any whole countrey or any more then the ſcope of a Citie, yet if wee might enioy trafficke and be aſſured of the ſame, wee might bee much inriched, our Naute might be increaſed, & a place of ſafetie might there be found, if change of religion or ciuill warres ſhoulde happen in this realme, which are thinges of great benefite. But if we may inioy any large Territorie of apt ſoyle, we might ſo vſe the matter, as we ſhould not dٍepende vpon Spaine for oyles, ſacks, reſinges, orenges, lemons, Spaniſh ſkinnes, &c. Nor vppon Fraunce for woad, bayſalt, and gaſcoyne wines, nor on Eſtlande for flaxe, pitch, tarre, maſtes, &c. So we ſhoulde not ſo exhauſt our treaſure, and ſo exceedingly inriche our doubtfull friendes, as we doe, but ſhoulde purchaſſe the commodities that we want for halfe the treaſure that now we do: but

ſhould

should by our own industries & the benefits of the soile there cheapely purches oyles, wines, salt, fruits, pitch, tarre, flaxe, hempe, mastes, boordes, fishe, gold, siluer, copper, tallowe, hides and many commodities: besides if there be no flatts to make salt on, if you haue plentie of wood you may make it in sufficient quantitie for common vses at home there.

If you can keepe a safe hauen, although you haue not the friendship of the neere neyghbours, yet you may haue trafficke by sea vpon one shore or other, vpon that firme in time to come, if not present.

If you finde great plenty of tymber on the shore side or vpon any portable riuer, you were best to cut downe of the same the first wynter, to bee seasoned for shippes, barkes, botes and houses.

And if neere such wood there be any riuer or brooke vpon the which a sawing mill may be placed, it woulde doe great seruice, and therefore consideration woulde bee had of suche place.

And if such port & chose place of setling were in possessiō & after fortified by art, although by ye land side our Englishmē were kept in, and might not inioy any traffick with the next neighbours, nor any vittel: yet might they vittel themselues of fishe to serue verie necessitie, and enter into amitie with the enemies of their next neighbours, & so haue vent of their marchandize of England and also haue vittel, or by meanes hereupon to be vsed to force the next neighbours to amitie. And keeping a nauie at the setling place, they shoulde finde out along the tracte of the lande to haue trafficke, and at diuers Ilandes also. And so this first seate might in tixte become a stapling place of the commodities of many countreys and territories, and in tyme this place myght become of all the prouinces round about the only gouernour. And if the place first chose should not so wel please our people, as some other more lately founde out: There might bee an easie remoue, and that might be rased, or rather kept for others of our nation to auoyde an ill neyghbour, &c.

If the soyles adioyning to such conuenient hauen and
setling

setling places be founde marshie and boggie, then men skil-
ful in draining are to be caried thither. For arte may worke
wonderfull effectes therein, and make the soyle rich for many vses.

To plante vppon an Ilande in the mouth of some notable riuer, or vpon the poynt of the lande entring into the riuer, if no such Iland be, were to great ende. For if such riuer
were nauigable or portable farre into the lande, then would
arise great hope of planting in fertill soyles, and trafficke on
the one or on thother side of the riuer, or on both, or the lin-
king in amitie with one or other petie king contēding there
for dominion.

Such riuers founde, both barges and boates may bee
made for the safe passage of such as shal perce ẙ same. These
to bee couered with doubles of course linnen artificially
wrought, to defend the arrow or the dart of the sauage from
the rower.

Since euery soyle of the world by arte may be made to
yeelde things to feede and to cloth man, bring in your returne a perfect note of the soyle without and within, and we
shall deuise if neede require to amende the same, & to draw it
to more perfectiō. And if you finde not fruits in your planting place to your liking, we shal in v. drifats furnish you wt
such kinds of plants to be caried thither ẙ winter after your
planting, as shall the very next summer folowing, yeeld you
some fruite, and the yere next folowing, as much as shal suffice a towne as big as Callice, and that shortly after shall be
able to yeeld you great store of strong durable good sider to
drinke, & these trees shalbe able to increase you within lesse
then vii. yeres as many trees presently to beare, as may suffice the people of diuers parishes, which at the first setling
may stand you in great steade, if the soyle haue not the commoditie of fruites of goodnesse already. And because you
ought greedily to hunt after thinges that yeelde present reliefe, without trouble of cariage thither, therefore I make
mencion of these, thus specially, to the ende you may haue it
specially in mynde.

FINIS.

The

The names of certaine commodities growing in part of America, not presently inhabited by any Christians frõ Florida Northward,

gathered out of the discourses, of *Verarzanus, Thorne,*
Cartier, Ribalt, Theuet, and best, which haue bin personal-
ly in those Countreys, and haue seene these things
amongst many others.

Beastes.

Leopardes.
Stagges.
Hartes.
Deare.
Beares.
Hares.
Wildeswine.
Connyes.
White beares.
A beast farre bigger then an oxe.
Wolues.
Dogges.
A kinde of beast like a Conny.
Beuers.
Marterns.
Foxes.
Bagers.
Otters.
Weesels.
A beast called Su being like a Bull.

Birdes.

Haukes.
Bitters.
Curlewes.
Herons.
Woodcockes.
Partridges.
Small birdes.
Plentie of foule for al pleasant game.
Apozates.
Blackbirdes.
Cranes.
Crowes like Cornish Choughes.
Duckes.
Godetes.
Geese.
Pigions.
Margaues.

Pheasants.

Swannes.
Thrushes.
Turtles.
Finches.
Nightingales. &c.

Fishes.

Coddes.
Salmons.
Seales.
Makerels.
Tortoyses.
Whales.
Horsefishes.
A fish like a grayhound good meate.
Lampreys.
Crabbes.
Crefishes.
Lobsters.
Eeles.
The riuers full of incredible store of all good fishe.

Wormes.

Silke wormes fayre and great.

Trees.

Bay.
Cypres.
Damson.
Palme.
Many trees yeelding sweet sauour.
Okes.
Nut trees.
Firre.
Uines.
Cahene good against poyson.
Cedars.   Hasell trees.
Cheritrees.   Walnuttrees.
Pepper trees.
Aneda which healeth many diseases.

K 4.   Ashe.

Aſhe. Elmes.
Boxe. Whitelmes.
Cidron. Pynes.
Yewe. Willowes.
Filbirdtrees better then ours.
Whitethornes bearing a berrie as big
    as a Damſon.
Vines bearing a great grape.

Fruites.

Cowcumbers. Guordes.
Cytrons. Mulberries.
Raſpis. Almonds.
Apples. Melons.
Damſons. Figges.
Reaſons great and ſmall.
Muſke melons. Lemons.
Orenges. Dates very great.
Strawberries.
Gooſeberries red and white.

Gummes.

Roſen. Pitche. Tarre.
Turpentine. Honnie.
Frankencenſe. Ware.

Spices and Drugges.

Pepper.
Small ſpices like to vire.
Reubarbe in Florida : diuerſe other
    kindes.

Hearbes and floures.

Many ſortes of herbes differing from
    ours.
Many ſimples like thoſe of Fraunce.
Hempe.
Parſeley.
    Redde.
Roſes. White.
    Damaſke.

Grayne and Pulſe.

Corne like Rie. Myllet.
Dates. Beanes of diuers
Peaſon. coulers.
Another ſtrãge corne of good nouriſh-
    ment.
Maiz.

Metalles.

Gold in good quantitie.
Siluer.
Coper.
Leade.
many bits they minerall matter.

Precious ſtones.

Turqueſes.
Rubies.
Pearles great and faire.
Precious ſtones of diuers colours.
Elurgni a ſtone much eſtemed there.
Kiph a kind of ſtone ſhining bright.

Other ſtones.

Marble very hard. Jaſper.
Alabaſter. Freeſtone.
Quarries of gliſtring ſtones.

Colours.

Yelowe. Redde.
Blewe. Scarlet.
    Roane colour.

Dear eſkinnes wrought like branched
    Damaſke.
Harts ſkinnes paynted and died of di-
    uers colours.
Bagges of red colours.
A roote called Auaty that they dye red
    withall in Florida.

*So as the commodities already knowen,
    beſides many yet vnknowen are
        theſe, and that in great
            quantitie.*

Fleſhe. Fruites.
Fiſhe. Grayne.
Beueradges or drink of diuers ſortes.
Golde. Copper.
Siluer. Lead.
Pearles. Furres.
Spices. Feathers.
Drugges. Gummes.
    Oyles.
Silke.
Hides vndreſſed.
Beaſts ſkins wrought like Damaſke.
Lether died.
Hartes ſkinnes painted.
Stones for fayre building.
Precious ſtones.
Colours.
All kinde of good wood.

Imprinted at London at the
*three Cranes in the Vine-
tree, by Thomas Daw-
ſon.* 1582.